Shaking Hands with the Devil

The Intersection of Terrorism and Theology

Shaking Hands with the Devil

The Intersection of Terrorism and Theology

William J. Abraham

HIGHLAND
LOCH PRESS
Dallas, TX

In memory of my beloved son

Timothy
(1971–2012)

who understood what
is at stake

Cover design by Chris Miller of **Rainmaker Advertising**

First edition
Published by Highland Loch Press
Dallas, Texas, USA

in association with

Wordsmith
Academic Press

a division of **Wordsmith Media Inc.**

ISBN: 978-0615708898

www.highlandlochpress.com

Contents

"Never shake hands with
the devil until you meet him!"
he advised his companion-on-the-road.
"Paddy," replied the
stranger, "*I* am the devil!"

From an old Irish folk-tale.

1
—

Massacre of the Innocents

Initial Description and Definition

Terrorism is a very nasty business.

It is not difficult to define what terrorism is. On the grand scale terrorism is the deliberate use of violence directed at innocent people, targeted at the few in order to influence the many or their leaders, designed for political purposes, perpetrated by a sub-national group or non-state entity that is organized with an identifiable chain of command or conspiratorial cell structure. While this is a mouthful, it worked well until the massacre of thirteen soldiers at Fort Hood, Texas, by the army psychiatrist, Major Nidal Hasan. More simply: terrorism is the use of violence against innocent people for political purposes. Of course, it is easy to quibble over this or that element in a definition. Sometimes quibbling deepens our insight and sharpens our intellectual tools. However, the simpler definition here serves my purposes admirably. Terrorism is simply the use of violence against innocent people for political purposes; it is the massacre of innocents for political gain.

A Graphic Example

Take the terrorist bomb in Enniskillen, Northern Ireland, on November 8, 1987. For years folk in the area had remembered their dead from two world wars with a parade through the town that climaxed with a church service. There was nothing hostile or adversarial in spirit about the occasion; there was to be a march up the town with the local, much-loved Ballyreagh Silver Band in the lead. Robin Emerson, a brilliant mind whom I counted as a friend at school, was the bandmaster, but he had forgotten his music, so the parade was delayed. The parade route is well known; the marchers wind their way up towards the war memorial in Belmore Street. The memorial stands right in front of the local convent school and close to McNulty's bicycle shop; it is an impressive sight. A soldier stands bowed close to two plaques with 836 names inscribed on them. A network of local folk stood against the wall of the empty hall across the road, sheltering from the cold westerly wind. The hall was a set of Reading Rooms, the property of St. Michael's parish, at the time used for bingo sessions and storage. A bag with forty pounds of explosives was carefully positioned on the first floor inside the gable wall against which the innocent were expected to be stationed. Usually the hall would have been searched; on this occasion the search had been omitted. Out of nowhere there was a blast. The bomb went off inside the empty hall, shattering the sheltering wall. When it was all over, eleven people were dead, sixty-three were injured, and the beautiful lakeland area was blown apart for years to come.

This area was home to me; I knew it intimately. I spent my teenage years in Enniskillen. I got my first bicycle from McNulty's shop when I gained a scholarship to Portora Royal School there. I had been converted to faith in the local Methodist church there during a bad bout of intellectual measles. I can still remember the spot outside the Salvation Army Hall on the Sligo Road where my teenage atheism fell apart and I became ripe for conversion. I found my first academic book in theology about the obscure Danish theologian from the nineteenth century, Soren Kierkegaard, in a book store one hundred yards from the war memorial. I left when it came time to go to Queen's University in Belfast to study French, philosophy, and psychology. I have taken tour groups to Enniskillen from Texas, and they have instantly loved the place. Enniskillen is a jewel in an area of stunning lakeland beauty.

I also knew many of the people who died. I caught the details on television in Dallas after coming home from church that morning. I can still see the bandsmen working in the rubble trying with bare hands to get to the dead and injured. I had been a member of the Ballyreagh Band as a teenager and loved every minute of my time with them. I had been trained on the tenor horn by the legendary, one legged-teacher, Tommy Watson, on Thursday evenings. Originally the band had been mounted on horseback; there is even an old photograph to prove it. By my time it was a wonderful experience to be part of it; it was serious about its music but not too serious. Suddenly a band of amateur musicians were forced to abandon their plans to play music in order to become medics, counselors, diggers with spades, and demolition workers. I watched the reports every hour, straining to see and hear the details.

One of the young people who died that day was Marie Wilson, whom I had known as a toddler in Sunday school. She died holding the hand of her father, Gordon Wilson, who himself was injured and became famous for his remarks about forgiveness that afternoon and for his later efforts to talk to the terrorists directly. Another casualty was Wesley Armstrong whom I had known in the church choir. I knew Johnny Megaw; he has always had a special place in my memory. His appearance matched the rawness of his name. He stood out in the town because of his Antrim accent, because of the bicycle that he rode all over the area, because of his rough externals, and, above all because of his zeal in the faith. Johnny was keen to share his lively convictions; he had a wily courage among people who were half-embarrassed by his enthusiasm; yet he was a lovable person; and everybody knew that he meant well. Johnny had died instantly in the rubble. He was sixty-seven, a retired painter, and had lived in Enniskillen for thirty-five years. Every Christmas he spent most of his earnings on gifts for the sick and elderly. Because of his simple generosity, Johnny now has a portrait in the geriatric wing of the Erne hospital. Many regretted that they took him back to county Antrim to bury him in the family plot in Ballymena; his brother took flak from a local businessman on this count. The same brother got a touching letter from a Roman Catholic nun who knew him. Fr. Brian D'Arcy, who had heard Johnny preach in the open air on the Diamond in Enniskillen when he was at school there, spoke fondly of him on national television on Dublin's *Late Late Show* in the week after the bomb.

The carnage in Enniskillen was the work of the Provisional IRA, the main terrorist organization in Ireland. Martin McGuiness at the highest levels of its inner courts is reported to have sanctioned it.[1]

---

[1] "Fermanagh units, seeking revenge for Loughgall and for the treatment of IRA funerals, were given permission by Martin McGuiness, who was in overall command

The total affair was a sophisticated operation that involved several brigades. No less than thirty people participated. The bomb had been manufactured across the border in the Ballinamore area of Co. Leitrim and had been assembled by the South Fermanagh Brigade. Prior to this two men in Enniskillen had gathered intelligence. Another briefed those who delivered the bomb on the layout of the area and on how to get in and out expeditiously. The bomb began its way to its final, destructive resting place on Friday night with the help of the West Fermanagh Brigade. To avoid detection en route, the journey was done in relays with scouts up front to make sure the roads were clear of road checks. By late Saturday or early Sunday, the bomb was put in place by a four-man bomb squad assisted by the two who had gathered intelligence. The caretaker of the hall and some friends who were playing cards downstairs heard mysterious creaking sounds upstairs. They paused; the noise stopped; one went to the door and called out; nothing happened; he returned to the card-game. At twenty to one in the morning one of them shouted: "If anybody's there, we're locking up." They locked the outside door that had been open all evening and went home to bed. The bomb inside was set to go off at exactly 10:43 the next morning.

The bomb exploded precisely on time. Immediately a column of smoke went up. The wall vibrated, erupted into the air, and then came down in large slabs on top of the people standing beside it. Bricks flew everywhere. Bodies were hurled into steel railings, leaving gruesome injuries. Panes of glass shattered along Belmore Street and cut into human flesh. There was a deadly silence before pandemonium set in. One woman's head was cracked open like a china doll, yet there was no blood and gore; the head was covered in gray dust. One man's big black overcoat was blown inside out. One boy could no longer feel his left leg below the knee; most of his front teeth were gone. Another saw his mother's face totally squashed, dead before him, close to his dying father. A man lost half his jaw, blood pouring out of it; the buttons were blown off his wife's coat and the shoes blown off her feet. As Monsignor Seán Cahill aptly said at St. Michael's Roman Catholic Church that morning, there

---

of both the Army Council and the Northern Command, to attack a number of Remembrance Day ceremonies in the hope of catching UDR or British Army personnel. Two were defused, but the third detonated, killing 11 civilians at the cenotaph in Enniskillen." See Liam Clarke and Kathryn Johnston, *Martin McGuiness: From Guns to Government* (Edinburgh: Mainstream Publishing, 2003), 189.

had been a massacre of the innocents.

The Bigger Picture

My interest in terrorism stems directly from living with it one way or another all my life. I have lived under the shadow of terrorism in that I was born and spent the formative years of my life in a world where terrorism was the bedrock order of the day. Thus growing up as a child in the fifties and sixties I vividly remember tales of terrorist acts. I recall hearing in the distance the bombing of Brookeborough Police station. I remember visiting my Uncle Tommy's home, which had been hit when a bridge next door was the site of a major bomb in the late fifties. I recall living next to neighbors (not just good but wonderful ones too) who were stalwart members of the IRA. In 1969 I came back from my honeymoon to the Donegal Road area of Belfast to live in an area that was one of the backbones of resistance against IRA activity. We had folk in the alleyway behind our house preparing petrol bombs. My mother in coming to visit us was absolutely shocked by the foul language of the youngsters. "In all my life," she sniffed, "I have never heard such bad language." She was even more shocked when she discovered they were making petrol bombs. In 1977 when I came back from graduate studies in Oxford I went to live and work in an area in north Belfast that had the worst murder rate in Western Europe. The church I served in the Glencairn housing estate was one of the sites where bodies were dumped in the wake of terrorist murders. The building across from the church was an illegal drinking *shebeen* run by Protestant paramilitary groups. On one occasion I had to hide one of my Sunday school teachers in the back of my car and speed out of the area because he was being pursued by folk who wanted to shoot him. My telephone was tapped by Protestant paramilitaries; I know because on one occasion they could not stand what I was saying to a colleague and broke in on the line to vent their rage. When my brother sacked an unreliable employee, the employee went to visit the local paramilitary thugs. In a week or so my brother's death was announced in the local papers as a form of intimidation; they were sending a clear message that his life was in danger; happily they did not follow through on their threat. Later a different network tied him up in his home and robbed him; he is still working through the aftereffects.

These episodes are simply the tip of an iceberg where family members were threatened, where friends were killed because they served in the police and prison services, and where parishioners lived under daily threat of death because they did simple things, like, sell necessary goods to the army or the police. My overall culture was shot through with murders, funerals, court-cases, bombings, acts of intimidation, marches, mafia-like activity, robberies, hatred, political shenanigans, and other countless events that shaped the culture to the core. The very geography I occupied was overlaid with a political, religious, and military map that took precedence over everything else. I first came to see the physical beauty of Ireland when I acted as an informal tour guide to one of my graduate students. He was a Ukrainian, but he had studied in Moscow. He wanted to visit Ireland because of his interest in Celtic Christianity; I wanted to see Russia because I had long ago fallen in love with her mystic, melancholy soul. We did a deal. I promised to show him Ireland and protect him, if he would do the same for me in Russia. The trip to Russia was unforgettable, but the journey around the North of Ireland even more so. I began to see Ireland through his eyes. It made me acutely aware of the political and religious color-coding that was second nature to me. Once I became aware of the coding, I could put it aside and see for the first time the extraordinary beauty of the coastline and countryside.

I had thought that in coming to North America I had left all this behind. When we came to live and work in the United States, I had deliberately chosen July 4 as the day of departure. Leaving Ireland was meant to be a kind of liberation from terrorism. 9/11 has changed all that. What I had lived with for years has become a standard feature of life in the West as a whole. In fact, watching current events is like shifting from a handheld screen to the big screen. What I had known on a small scale has become a worldwide reality. The news I now hear every evening on television and radio is depressingly similar to what I heard for years in Ireland. There is a steady catalogue of bombings, arrests, security alerts, interviews with experts, and press conferences.

It is not surprising that radical Islamists have been paying close attention to what happened in Northern Ireland. As Michael Gove has noted:

> Britain's handling of its domestic terrorist problem in the nineties was watched with great interest by Islamists. It reinforced

their view that while the West, as a whole, was decadent, there were particular weaknesses in Britain's political landscape that provided prospects for advance.

The attention with which Islamists monitored events in Northern Ireland was confirmed by one of Abu Musab al-Zarquawi's lieutenants in an interview with *Time* magazine when he asserted that the Irawui insurgency was encouraged in its efforts by the example of Northern Ireland. It didn't matter how much the West protested it was in the conflict for the long haul. Britain's response to Irish republicanism showed once again that Western nations didn't have the stomach for protracted campaigns, whatever the rhetoric uttered by Western leaders. If terrorists persist, terrorism will pay off.[2]

In reflecting with friends from Northern Ireland on terrorism we often felt part of a beleaguered minority who found no sympathy in the wider world. Ordinary decent citizens were hammered on a daily basis by sophisticated terrorists and their allies. They got money and moral backing from the United States. In the early 1980s, while working in Seattle, I got a letter from the commander in chief of the IRA in the state of Washington after I had given a lecture on the Irish situation in Bellevue at the public library; he clearly wanted me to know that he had gotten my name and address. I stopped giving lectures of that sort because of concerns about retaliation on family members back home. The IRA had all the necessary connections to pull the trigger. They also had a brilliant propaganda machine that exploited the code words of inclusivism, justice, peace, freedom, self-determination, national and ethnic identity, and the like, to the hilt. The victims and targets of terrorists were portrayed as bigoted, prejudiced, discriminatory, and intolerant. Ordinary, decent people were systematically demonized for political purposes. The terrorists and their leaders were portrayed as freedom fighters, heroes, poets, literary artists, and paragons of moral virtue. Even when I was a student at Oxford back in the 1970s, the English wanted little or nothing to do with Northern Ireland because of the image they had picked up from the airwaves. I once took a parcel to the local post office to send back home; the postal agents insisted on filling out a customs form; they thought that Northern Ireland was a foreign country.

What has astonished me since 9/11 is that the moral oxygen that gave cover to terrorist acts in Northern Ireland was suddenly sucked

[2]Michael Gove, *Celsius 7/7* (London: Weidenfield and Nicholson, 2006), 46–47.

out of the air. There is and will continue to be a very hotly contested debate about terrorism now that it has gone global and ballistic. However, the atmosphere has radically changed. I now find a host of writers and commentators who give voice to the intuitions and concerns (and the confusion too) that I knew in my bones for years but never took the time to articulate. I also find that the issues as they arose in Northern Ireland are mirrored in the debate about global terrorism now. The comment of the distinguished historian Michael Burleigh captures the mood perfectly:

> Initially, I regarded this [Northern Ireland] as an almost inexplicable, atavistic, tribal struggle fitfully audible as distant bombs rattled the windows of various places I've lived in London. However, in the long term this squalid little conflict anticipated the sinister surrender of power to so-called 'moderate' community leaders (and the creation of exceptional pockets where law does not appear to apply) that is becoming evident in the responses of European governments to the much wider threat of Islamic radicalism.[3]

We have to be careful in making the move from Ireland to the wider international scene, but there are obvious analogies and insights to be explored.

An Initial Question

The initial issue to be addressed is this: why does terrorism trouble us so much? Is our preoccupation something drummed up by a sensation driven media and by clever politicians, or does terrorism carry within it a cluster of issues that keep us awake when we think of them? The second option is the more compelling. In fact, so many issues are attached to terrorism that we need to narrow the range of focus in order to keep our nerve. I shall work through a cluster of four reasons why we are so troubled by terrorism.

The Moral Challenge

We can begin with the moral challenges terrorism presents.

Initially everything is plain sailing. Terrorism is intrinsically evil. It is an unmitigated evil. The Remembrance Day bombing in Enniskillen was an act of vicious violence carried out with cunning and deliberation against a group of innocent civilians. There is no way in which it can be morally justified; there are no extenuating cir-

---

[3] Michael Burleigh, *Sacred Causes: The Clash of Religion and Politics, from the Great War to the War on Terror* (New York: HarperCollins, 2007), xiv.

cumstances to mitigate its brutality. Politic
or any agents of violent change, any and all wh
acts of violence involved or who try to cover the
ation in a fog of rhetoric are morally corrupt. They
moral virginity and have destroyed their conscience.
the matter is clear: a heinous act of evil was done.

Every effort to turn aside from this judgment is itself
evil. Of course, terrorists will never accept the standard conc
terrorism we now deploy or the moral evaluation that goes w
it because it is in their interest to cause confusion and obscurity
Concealment and self-deception are the housemates of terrorism.
Terrorism is the tip of a network of moral evils that grow and in-
terbreed like parasites on each other. Hence the very term itself
gets caught up in the conflict. Happily, ordinary people can see
through this, for it is average, ordinary people who are the victims
of terrorism. It is decent, everyday people who pay their taxes, raise
their children, go to work, and mind the store who are the primary
targets.

So it is no surprise that ordinary people are troubled by terrorism. However, our trouble with terrorism cuts deeper than mere
indignation at an intrinsic evil. Think of terrorism as a border
crossing. Once you cross the line, all sorts of things up to this line
become permissible. Lying, intimidation, extortion, torture, bank-
robbery, betrayal, drug running, group infighting, misplaced zeal,
propaganda, economic disruption, civil chaos, and rationalization
become live options. Options that were unthinkable beforehand
now become possible. If we can kill scores of innocent people with
small bombs and bullets, then the move to dirty bombs and biological weapons is merely one of degree. The restraints are off and the
race to the world of the apocalyptic is on. Aleksandr Solzhenitsyn
captured the problem aptly.

> Physics is aware of phenomena which occur only at *threshold*
> magnitudes, which do not exist at all until a certain *threshold*
> encoded by and known to nature has been crossed...Evidently
> evildoing also has a threshold magnitude. Yes, a human being
> hesitates and bobs back and forth between good and evil all his
> life. He slips, falls back, clambers up, repents, things begin to
> darken again. But just so long as the threshold of evildoing is
> not crossed, the possibility of returning remains, and he himself
> is still within reach of our hope. But when, through the density
> of evil actions, the result either of their own extreme degree or

ddenly crosses that thresh-
without, perhaps, the pos-

concealed; they can be re-
_eans to good ends. It also
n others. Terrorists think
ey are organized in small
seek each other out like
intercourse and marital
ain, Colonel Gadafi in
__rs from the girlfriends
__ Palestinian and Israeli flags and sym-
____d on walls in Belfast. Bystanders and states are readily
tooled into paying to keep the brothels open. Collections are taken up outside churches. Money is siphoned off from charities and government agencies. Next of kin separated by generations in faraway lands are tricked into sending millions of dollars for the cause. Grand narratives of mythic heroes are invented and kept alive; history is rewritten; cultures are poisoned; memorials, marches and festivals are organized; new generations are indoctrinated; political life is wrecked. Terrorists groups breed new terrorist groups, who terrorize each other. So the IRA gives birth to the Provisional IRA, who give birth to the Real IRA and to the Continuity IRA; by action at a distance these provoke the creation of the UVF and the UDA with their numerous offspring. Only experts can keep up with the illegitimate birth announcements and names. Then the bastard offspring multiply. A group of skinheads in Dresden have set up a German C Company in honor of the loyalist terrorist leader, Johnny Adair. The leader, Nick, has had one of Adair's slogans, 'Simply the Best', tattooed across his back. The loyalist cause has now spread to the German Fatherland.

I have used high-octane language in my moral evaluation of terrorism. This often evokes nervousness, not least among intellectuals. Some want to avoid the language of good and evil altogether. In fact, Richard Bernstein, one of the best philosophers of the last generation, castigates the ready use of the language of good and evil

[4]Edward E. Ericson and Daniel J. Mahoney, eds., *The Solzhenitsyn Reader: New and Essential Writings, 1947–2005* (Wilmington, DE.: ISI Books, 2006), 235. The emphasis is as in the original.

as an abuse of evil. Bernstein is also worried about the mentality on display. He contrasts the mentality of fallible pragmatism with the mentality of moral absolutes.[5] In my description of terrorism we have just stepped into a world of moral absolutes; and if that is the case (he contends), we need to reach for immediate protection. Moral absolutists worry us for a host of reasons. Moral absolutists smell of certainty; they are impervious to reason; they are self-righteous and intolerant; they are exploitative and manipulative; they are dualistic and paranoiac. "God help us all," (we are told) if powerful politicians take to using strong moral language. Moral relativists go one step further. All our moral evaluations are relative to our time and culture; they are not categorical or universal; they apply only to our personal constructed world and not to every possible world; they are really clever cover-ups for power and status. So we should lighten the tone, set the moral thermostat a bit lower, and relax.

I disagree. Terrorism is like rape in that it is intrinsically evil. Moral debate and perception at this point runs deep. Any counter-moral claim or ethical theory that runs afoul of this particular moral perception should be rejected as false and inadequate. We should reject moral relativism precisely because it calls into question the evil of terrorism. Moral relativism is intellectually bankrupt as a response to terrorism, for it cannot cope with the intensity of the evil we are facing. Attempts to lessen the horror of terrorism are signs of intellectual disease. Either we have a bad argument on our hands, or, we are covertly in favor of the ends terrorists seek to accomplish, or we are not functioning intellectually with a full deck of cards. So we should keep our nerve. Keeping our nerve does not mean that we are impervious to reason, infallible, manipulative, self-righteous, and the like. It simply means we are standing by the light we possess. If this is moral absolutism, then two cheers for moral absolutism. We are deeply troubled by the moral evil of terrorism; so we should be.

We can take this one step further. Our visceral reaction to terrorism as a horrendous evil is an instance where our passions instruct our reason. As Edmund Burke noted, "we behold such disasters in the moral as we should behold a miracle in the physical order of

[5]Richard J. Bernstein, *The Abuse of Evil: The Corruption of Politics and Religion Since 9/11* (Malden, Mass: Polity Press, 2005), chap. 1.

things. We are alarmed into reflection; our minds (as it has long since been observed) are purified by terror and pity; our weak, unthinking pride is humbled under the dispensations of a mysterious wisdom."[6]

The Practical Challenge

We are also deeply troubled by the fact that terrorism is devilishly frustrating to contain much less eradicate.

As soon as we solve one set of problems another one pops up; we dodge one bullet and another one is close behind. The immediate response is to tackle the challenge of damage control. We have to attend to the wounded, bury the dead, open up the roads, and do what we can to get back to normal life. The medium term challenge is preventative and focuses on how to stop planned terrorist attacks. We have to set up security systems, reform the intelligence services, and go after determined enemies. These efforts can only deter; they cannot prevent. In the long-term, we have to change the cultural background music, figure out what to do with captured terrorists, and sort out how best to help the victims.

Teams of agents are involved in the response to terrorism: police officers, soldiers, medical staff, clergy, scholars, journalists, lawyers, and politicians. We worry about the ability of our leaders. Are they sufficiently informed? What do they really know? Do they have the requisite wisdom and patience? Will they have the courage to withstand the pressures? Will they hesitate until it is too late? Will they over-react? Will they over-simplify? How will their political convictions and ideologies fill in the inevitable gaps in knowledge and judgment? How will they muster the skill to pull together the factions and groups who must cooperate if we are to find solutions that can be implemented?

We worry about the costs, as billions of dollars are diverted to fund a host of new initiatives. We know that millions of dollars will be wasted, or stolen, or mismanaged. We realize that some people will benefit financially and that these financial interests will find their way into our politics. We recognize that politicians of every party and sect will have to factor terrorism into every calculation they make. We also know that it is extremely difficult to get things right first time around and that opponents will pounce on any and

[6]Edmund Burke, *Reflections on the Revolution in France* (London: Penguin, 1986), 175.

every mistake to claw their way into political office.

In Northern Ireland the terrorism of the late 1950s fizzled out of its own accord in 1962. Like most of my generation I was relatively optimistic that we could find a way forward out of the troubles when I went up to Queen's University, Belfast, in 1966. That optimism was built on illusion. I had paid sporadic attention to debates in the student union and had voted strategically on the issue of the timing of civil rights marches. I knew that marches would descend into rioting, especially so when they were timed to coincide with the closing of the Belfast shipyards when the workers were leaving for home. I recall a vigorous debate about the timing of a protest march directed at discrimination, electoral arrangements, civil rights, and other such items. Some wanted to march at 5.00 p.m. because they were politically on the left and wanted naively to join hands with the shipyard workers and begin ushering in the revolution. Others voted for 5.00 p.m. because they wanted a confrontation with Protestant workers that would cause sufficient unrest to bring down the state. I voted strategically for marches that would begin at 2.00 p.m. rather than 5.00 p.m.; and then I headed back to my books in the library. In reality I was much more interested in my studies, for education was its own way up and out of the "stupid troubles", as we called them. So I was taken aback in 1969 when violence erupted in earnest. By the early seventies terrorism had taken hold across the board.

The cost of meeting the bill has been staggering. Billions of pounds have been paid out to cover compensation, fix buildings, train security personnel, maintain military operations, house prisoners, fund medical care, and the like. Sorting out political differences has also been costly not just financially but emotionally and intellectually. Initially fresh and radical proposals surfaced in the political underworld. The core issue was how to bring the warring factions together politically in one set of civic institutions where power-sharing would be the order of the day. Attempts to impose such arrangements in the seventies were smashed by strikes. So the war continued unabated. A second attempt at imposition ten years later was defeated by electoral means. By the early nineties, the IRA pretty much knew it could not win militarily. Secret agents had infiltrated the command structure right to the very top. One of them, the son of an Italian immigrant to Belfast, was affectionately known as "Steak knife" and the "Nutter". He was in charge of disciplining wayward terrorists, so he had to know of every approved operation and could pass on this information to the security forces. Consequently, the IRA was hopelessly compromised from a military point of view. In any case, the resolve to resist terrorism was as strong as ever; ordinary people are incredibly resilient. In the meantime, the British government made it clear publicly that its commitment to Northern Ireland was driven merely by prudence rather than loyalist policy.

In time power-sharing was embraced by the moderate, majority parties from the Unionist and Nationalist communities. With massive outside intervention that spread from Dublin, to London, to Brussels, and across the Atlantic to the White House, these flexible parties did the necessary heavy-lifting to get relatively normal politics off the ground. All the way it was a case of five steps forward and three backwards. In the Belfast Agreement signed on Good Friday, April 10, 1998, the hard-line Sinn Féin party had no option but to come on board. In the meantime the Rev. Dr. Paisley and the Democratic Unionist Party did all they could to undermine the agreement and to knock off the moderate Unionists at election time. The Assembly in Belfast started and stopped. Salaries and expense accounts remained in place; the trough of the public purse was kept replenished for hungry snouts; think tanks and conferences were formed and funded. Archbishop Desmond Tutu, tempted to play the messiah once again, showed up with his peace and reconciliation circus. After all that they had achieved, the moderate parties were soundly beaten at the polls by the hardliners in 2007. Those who were crucial to making peace possible were thoroughly marginalized by political enemies who gladly helped themselves to the spoils they had at one time rejected. David Trimble of the Ulster Unionist Party and John Hume of the Social Democratic and Labour Party were given the Nobel Peace Prize in 1998 and then sent home to read, play with the dog, listen to classical music, and watch television. The Rev. Dr. Ian Paisley became the leading elected Protestant Politician in Northern Ireland. Having defeated all his political enemies by ruthlessly crushing them for deal making with the enemy, he eventually made a deal with Sinn Féin, the political wing of the IRA. Not surprisingly many of his followers are heartbroken, for they know full well that Paisley is engaged in a massive reversal.

Even the winners have a price to pay. His wife was a critical factor in his decision to make the deal in which he turned his own world upside down. In the meantime many of the major political actors still need bulletproof windows and bodyguards.

If the cumulative costs for containing and eliminating Irish terrorism were added up, the bill would be staggering. Even then, we have our doubts about the outcome. The practical challenge remains alive in Northern Ireland. That practical challenge multiplies beyond calculation when we move to the global terrorism we now face. No wonder we are troubled.

The Religious Challenge

We are also deeply troubled by the connection between terrorism and religion.

Understanding terrorism is an intellectual nightmare. We have to be ruthlessly specific and particular. There is no general explanation or causal theory that will capture what is at stake in Italy's Red Brigades, Germany's Baader-Meinhof Gang, Peru's Sendero Luminoso, Mozambique's Renamo, Sri Lanka's Tamil Tigers, al-Qaeda, Ireland's Irish Republican Army, or Northern Ireland's Ulster Defense Association. In December 2005 there were 189 groups, entities, and individuals in the list of terrorists and groups identified in Executive Order 133244. Different governments have different lists. Global theories that draw on such vague notions as poor education, religious fanaticism, the irrationality of faith, American imperialism, globalization, the collision of mentalities, and the clash of civilizations are close to worthless as explanatory tools. Terrorist acts are as specific as the causes they represent, the personalities that perform them, the motives that drive them, and the contexts in which they take place. All our understanding is underdetermined, contested, provisional, and incomplete. Yet we must do what we can to understand them. In the case of both Irish and global terrorism religion is an ineradicable factor. This is deeply troubling intellectually.

The killing in Enniskillen was sectarian. All the people who were killed were Protestants. Six were Presbyterians, three were Methodists, and two were Church of Ireland or Irish Anglicans. Every single one of them was a serious believer. The funerals were attended by thousands of Catholics and Protestants; the subsequent efforts across the religious divide to come together are impressive. However, the religious dimension is inescapable. When Sister Anne Marie, a nun from the nearby convent and the respected Principal of St. Franchea's girls' school, came to the scene, the wife of one of the injured roundly chastised her. It was obnoxious, the wife insisted, to be aided by an agent of the religious enemy. There was nothing personal in this, to be sure; the matter was one of six hundred years of history. "Oh God," thought Sister Anne Marie, "she is linking me with what happened." The links are tangled.

The Rev. Ivan Foster, a Free Presbyterian minister in the area, published an article shortly after the massacre, and had fifty thousand copies distributed. He attacked the police for not searching the building; he laid into the main Protestant churches for being ecumenical; he chastised the visiting government officials for having blood on their hands. The ultimate enemy was Rome, whose liturgies misled the people about their eternal salvation, whose local leaders had failed to give adequate assistance to the police, and whose international leaders were in a war to destroy Ulster Protestantism, the last bastion of true religion in the world. Yet Foster went further. He quoted Amos 3:6: "Shall there be evil in the city and God hath not done it?" Were we to believe that God had been the real agent behind it all? Had God killed all those innocent citizens in order to bring the people of Ulster to their senses? Is this how we are to understand terrorist acts?

Foster prevaricated at this point. God in his sovereignty allowed it to happen; it was a case of permission rather than direct action. God was afflicting his people for the errors of ecumenism in order to promote repentance and reformation. All those who died were Christian believers. So Foster noted that God had taken away believers rather than unbelievers. He then suggested that God had come to fight unbelieving Ulster by permitting the killing of Christian believers. For the moment Ulster remains undefeated; her political sovereignty remains intact; but she will be defeated, if the Almighty takes up arms against her and comes after the unbelievers. Hence it was time to turn away from ecumenism and Rome, to give up apostate Protestantism and empty ritualism, and to turn to holiness and purity through his version the gospel.

Foster's position represents one end of the theological spectrum. It is a mistake to dismiss him as a fanatical idiot driven by emotion. Historically, he sees acts of terrorism as a continuation of the post-

Reformation wars of religion. Moreover, he clearly reads the total situation in theological categories. Theologically, terrorism involves double agents, the divine and human providentially woven together in a seamless garment. This heady mix of historical and theological explanation gives everybody a pain in the brain. Religion and theology have bombed their way back into the public square. We simply do not have the categories to cope intellectually. Beyond that we do not know what to do with religious factors as they relate to terrorism. We feel we are slipping into a subterranean world of emotion, fanaticism, and irrationality.

Of course, we have in hand secular theories that shut down the conversation and eliminate theological considerations as off limits; there are many such theories currently available in the market. However, salient forms of terrorism challenge this strategy at its foundations in that they call into question all forms of secularism. We have all been so house-trained to exclude theology from politics that when it shows up we want to send it packing immediately. We thought that the issue was settled: politics is a public affair; religion is a private affair. Maybe the poor Paddies and poor Billies in Ireland have not gotten the message, but in time they will grow up and become enlightened. Paddy and Billy, however, will not be so easily silenced. They are now joined by militant, Islamic Puritans who have strange, unpronounceable names and very different accents; and they draw on an even older tradition of thought and practice. They are not afraid of modern forms of secularism and liberalism. They echo all too clearly some of the issues that are part of the history of Christianity. Truth be told, they expose blind spots in our political thinking that are scary and that can no longer be ignored. It is no wonder we are troubled by terrorism; it is hitched to religion; with one we get the other. Fanaticism has arrived; our teeth are on edge.

The Existential Challenge

We are also troubled by the spiritual and existential challenge posed by terrorism.

So long as terrorism is far away in remote places, we can continue our routines as usual. Unless we have some kind of personal connection we can readily go back to normal life. Every time we visit an airport we now know that this is an illusion. Terrorism by nature is a random act of violence that can hit anyone, anywhere. We know that the odds are low that we ourselves will be hit, but the security we took for granted in a civilized society is gone forever. We know that once we factor in weapons of mass destruction, then the effects will be catastrophic.

The threat of terrorism crops up in places where we do not expect it. When word came through that it was highly likely that Southern Methodist University would be chosen as the site for the President George W. Bush library, museum, and policy institute, I got an e-mail from two colleagues soliciting signatures that would oppose its coming. Given what I knew of their intellectual and political sensibilities, this was not a surprise. I was fascinated by one of the initial arguments they deployed. They claimed that if we got the library then the university and our students would automatically become terrorist targets. So it would be fine for rival universities and their students to be targets of terrorism; while we remained safe in Dallas, it would be all right to kill the Baptists down the road at Baylor University in Waco, the rival site for selection. What is interesting, however, is that there is real truth buried in the original proposition. In fact, I already knew that security would be a major issue. I was aware from the grapevine that it was already agreed that a guard would have to be posted at the digging of every hole in the ground in order to ensure that no explosives could be secretly planted and detonated later when they were filled in with the columns that would be part of the buildings. The issue here is not just a rerun of the problem of coping with the practical challenges of terrorism, it is that we now live with the prospect that we ourselves might get killed.

The existential dilemma is not just that we become acutely aware of our mortality; we also become aware of the evil in our own souls that can lie below the surface. If we think about it seriously, we can become acutely aware that we ourselves could be sucked into acts of terrorism. In my own case, this was, of course, highly unlikely given my family history and my upbringing. Yet friends tease that I even eat chocolate bars aggressively. I can easily see how a series of chance experiences could have drawn me into the underworld of violence represented by terrorism. Suppose I had had close friendships with political fanatics, that I had been immersed in conspiracy theories about opponents, and that I had been beaten up by thugs from the other side. It would have been easy to join up and serve the cause with enthusiasm.

We like to think of terrorists as different from ourselves, driven by poverty, bad ideologies, or experiences of oppression. However, terrorists turn out to be terribly normal. Many of them are nice people in private; they are very well educated; they take readily to their work over time. Indeed they can become accustomed to killing; in some cases abandoning it is extremely difficult. If we pay attention we realize that we are not the fine people we think we are; human agents are exceptionally vulnerable and liable to corruption. Consider the testimony of the lead mistress of one of the principal loyalist terrorists in Belfast, Johnny "Mad Dog" Adair.

> I drank and socialized with murderers, but I was in love with a man who was kind and caring and I didn't see hatred or anger in him at all. It may sound sad, unbelievable, but for a long time I found Johnny Adair and his friends very good people. They were ordinary, average, fun-loving, trustworthy and dedicated, except for the fact that they killed.[7]

Adair was well known for running errands for the elderly, bringing candy to the children on the streets, and giving money to the homeless. He had as many mattress appointments with adoring women as he could physically handle. He kept a large tank of tropical fish. Yet he was a ruthless terrorist leader.

Our sense of our own darkness deepens once we start reading around the topic. Some terrorists justify their terrorism by piling up lists of terrorist acts perpetuated by the West, beginning with what happened in World War II with the systematic carpet-bombing carried out not just against Dresden but right across Germany and beyond. To be sure, we can immediately distinguish between acts of terrorism committed within the context of war and acts of terrorism carried out for political purposes. Fine. However, the line can be hard to draw, and we must now face the fact that in times of war we ourselves, or our children and grandchildren, could be conscripted into acts of terrorism. Such thought experiments rattle our sense of ourselves as human agents. Terrorism is no longer a distant, public phenomenon, it has invaded our own intimate, spiritual space.

Terrorism drives us to think deeply about the human situation. Aren't there better ways to resolve disputes that this? Why can't

[7]June Caldwell and Jackie "Legs" Robinson, *In Love with a Mad Dog* (Dublin: Gill & Macmillan, 2006), v.

we rely on reason and good sense? If we can develop wonderful technology, how come we end up using it to wipe out innocent neighbors? Did we not come of age in modern history? Wasn't modernity all about the discovery of human dignity? Didn't we have an Enlightenment where we discovered the wisdom of solving our problems by negotiation, law, and democratic procedures? Are we now going back to a new Dark Ages? How can there be such appalling cruelty? We know we are not angels; are we now painfully discovering that we are brutal animals? Are we demons? And if anything remotely like that is the case, where can we find hope, now that we have left redemption and religion behind? Are we not opening the doors again to the crackpot evangelists on television who are already claiming that God has spoken to them about impending terrorist acts?[8]

The nasty business of terrorism has just gotten nastier.

---

[8]In January 2007 Pat Robertson publicly announced after a prayer retreat that in late 2007 a massive terrorist attack would strike the United States resulting in mass killing.

2

—

Orange and Green

Terrorism and Religion

It is strange that terrorism should be connected in any way, shape, or form to religion.

Religion is assumed to be about love and peace rather than violence and terror. The history of terrorism shows otherwise, of course, in that zealots, assassins, and thugs were names originally coined to identify terrorists who were also deeply religious. However, that was long ago. In any case, with Ireland (we say to ourselves) we are not dealing with any old religion; we are dealing with true religion. True religion in this instance is Christianity in its purest Catholic and Protestant forms, for where else but in God's own Ireland would these be found. Surely in holy Ireland, the land of saints and scholars, there cannot be any robust connection between religion and terrorism. A religious terrorist is an oxymoron. So we quickly want to dismiss terrorists as false believers, or as apostates, in order to keep violence at a safe distance. No true Christian believer could ever stoop to kill innocent civilians for political purposes. If they do this kind of thing, something must have gone badly wrong somewhere in the religion. Their religion must be false or malfunctioning; it must really be idolatry or blasphemy.

We can run this observation in the opposite direction. If we really understand terrorism we will also understand that terrorists could not really be religious. So we reach for descriptions of terrorists that will remove the contradiction. We think of terrorists as misguided idealists who have been driven to action by some great injustice, grievance, or oppression; they are really freedom fighters. In this case some might even allow that they are true believers motivated by a genuinely prophetic tradition, but this is a very risky stretch. More commonly we want to think of terrorists as nuts, thugs, criminals, lunatics, gangsters, or the tools of social and economic forces. In this instance we no longer see terrorists as agents; they are really patients, victims of this or that passion, flaw, and historical force. At the limit we may well be dealing with evil incarnate.

In the Irish situation, it was not difficult to find both strategies rolling around in the back of the mind. This was certainly my experience. I was aware of the dissonance and felt it acutely from time to time. Yet it was easy to resolve the pain in the brain by trying one or other of these ploys or even both of them together. True religion could not involve terrorism, and terrorists could not truly be religious. There was lots of encouragement for these options on hand from all mainline Christian leaders who constantly drew attention in public statements to the irreconcilability of terrorism and the Christian faith. They were clearly defending themselves and their religion; they were also hoping that declarations of pious, religious assemblies would make a difference. They all unceasingly called for peace and reconciliation.

Even the Rev. Dr. Ian Paisley, who became the First Minister in the Assembly in Belfast and a firebrand until his late conversion to serving in government with Sinn Féin, was committed to peace and reconciliation in his own inimitable way. Not, of course in the terms in which it was deployed by ecumenical church leaders. Those who talked like them on peace and reconciliation, he thundered, were deluded. If they were Protestant clergy, they were dupes of Rome; such discourse on Protestant lips is really a cover for a sellout to the enemy. If they were politicians they were living in political fantasy land, for there could not be reconciliation with the ideology of Irish nationalism. However, back then Paisley was generally perceived as a crackpot fundamentalist, a demagogue, and a self-serving politician, so his views could be set aside. He was not the Prince Charming he later became. He had developed his own partisan version of the Christian faith; his noisy, preachy accent sent shivers down the spine. I remember vividly attending a service he conducted with his usual gusto in Enniskillen. Afterwards the best word to describe how I felt was "soiled"; so much so that I dropped off in the town of Portadown on my way to Belfast and attended another service that Sunday just to cleanse my soul. In any case, Paisley at that time was a marginal figure; so the strategy of seeing him as sub-Christian worked perfectly. Even then Paisley was very careful to steer clear of terrorism. He could cleverly brandish the threat of violence when needed, but he was resolutely opposed to terrorism and made his views abundantly clear. So he shared the general conviction that true religion could not involve terrorism, and terrorists could not truly be religious.

My conversion within Irish Methodism as an inquisitive and restless teenager reinforced the claim that terrorists could not be true believers. Let me elaborate. When I came to faith I did not know that I was supposed to be bored reading John Wesley, the founder of Methodism in the eighteenth century, so his sermons provided a take on the faith that resolutely put love of God and neighbor at its very core. Equally important, Wesley had such a high standard of what it was to be Christian that it was easy to dismiss departure from it as merely nominal faith or dead orthodoxy. Moreover, Methodism came late in the day, so it has never engaged in killing or coercion; the very thought of doing so shows that one is not a true believer. Methodists are inescapably nice people for the most part; there are too few of them in Ireland to be a threat to anyone. They even have a slogan to capture the pacific side of their self-identity that goes right back to John Wesley, their founder: "Methodists are the friends of all and the enemies of none." I experienced this firsthand within Methodism in an area where the hard edge of the Presbyterian tradition was a minority report and where the aristocratic respectability of the Anglican tradition reinforced the Methodist ethos of grace and kindness.

So growing up I had beguiling ways of sorting through the relation between religion and terrorism. Yet there were other experiences that indirectly called such strategies into question and suggested that religion leaked extensively into politics and vice versa. If religion can leak into politics, and politics can leak into violence and terrorism, then maybe there is a real connection between religion and terrorism in Ireland after all. Anyone aware of developments in Christianity across the early centuries in the Roman Empire will be aware of the possibilities.

Certainly, religion was connected to politics in the Ireland I knew. I noted immediately that Protestants in my area voted one way and Catholics another. I saw that Catholics looked to Dublin and the Republic of Ireland as their capital and country; Protestants looked to London and the United Kingdom as theirs. I watched Catholics on the bus to school cross themselves as we passed a Protestant graveyard at a little crossroads called Pubble on the road between Tempo and Enniskillen. When I asked about this it was rumored that nationalist rebels were buried there for some strange reason; not even death separated religion from politics. The dawning of consciousness involved an immediate sense that religion and politics were Siamese twins. However, that sense became explicit in my teenage years. Allow me to explain.

Northern Ireland in the 1950s and 60s was saturated with religion. I was brought up as ethnically Protestant and nominally Methodist. My father had been killed in a terrible accident on the Tempo Road outside Enniskillen. He had climbed up into the back of a cattle truck behind the cabin in order to make room for extra passengers. Nobody anticipated that this would put him at great risk when they came to the railway bridge on the outskirts of the town. He was struck on the head and died on the spot. My mother, who did not sleep for fourteen nights, managed to bring up six boys on her own. My oldest brother had to stay off school for three months to take care of the farm. The care of the church was crucial to our material welfare, so going to Sunday school was normal. It was also an adventure when four to five of us managed to get on one bicycle on the road to our tiny local church in the village of Clabby. We figured out a way to use every conceivable perch on it. The spiritual care of the clergy was exemplary but in my case initially not very effective, for I had tried being a believer when I was ten and found it impossible to sustain at home. Faith and reason lost the battle with peer pressure, emotion, and imagination. Beyond that I encountered religion every single day in the opening assemblies of every school I attended and in the required instruction given in religion classes.

A Concrete Example

I first explicitly noted the relation between religion and politics in the Remembrance services that were held every year to honor the dead from the two World Wars. National identity was carefully woven inside a tapestry of faith. The tapestry was literal in the local Church of Ireland Cathedral, St. Macartin's, where the banners and colors of various Irish regiments hung from the walls. The connection between religion and politics really struck home, however, when I was initiated into the Orange Order as part of the normal routine of puberty.

The Orange Order was founded in 1795 after the Battle of the Diamond in Loughgall, Co. Armagh, between the Catholic Defenders and the Protestant Peep O'Day Boys over trading rights that left eighty dead. It borrowed heavily from the Freemasons; so I have often thought of the Orange Order as "Freemasonry for Dummies." In time the Order got the informal backing of the government, even though it was officially banned between 1823 and 1845. It became the DNA of political Protestantism, so much so that it was instrumental in the founding of the Unionist Party in 1886. Over the years it has been in effect a political ideology in a religious costume; the religion is Protestant, the political ideology is British constitutional nationalism as enshrined in the British Act of Settlement of 1701.

Irish nationalism has its mirror image of the Orange Order in the Ancient Order of Hibernians. In fact the founders of the Orange Order may have taken a cue from this older, rival cousin. The Ancient Order of Hibernians was founded in the 1560s as a bulwark against English settlers and as a defense of the Catholic faith. For a time it saw itself as a continuation of the 1641 rebellion, a Catholic uprising which attempted to wipe out heresy and the Protestant plantations of Ireland. By 1914 it saturated the whole island of Ireland and resolutely opposed any concessions to Protestant Ulster. After 1916 many of its members joined Sinn Féin and the IRA. There are still many branches in Ulster; they have an annual parade in Ballymena in August. Its largest membership is now in the United States where it coordinates the St. Patrick's Day Parade in New York City. Not surprisingly it has drawn criticism for being exclusively Irish Republican and wholly Catholic in its symbols and themes.

Growing up, the Orange Order was a recurring but not constant presence in my life. I attended the local parades and the Twelfth of July celebrations and enjoyed the music and spectacle of it all.[9] For

---

[9] The Twelfth of July was the day set aside to celebrate the victory of the Protestant King William over the Roman Catholic King James in 1690. It is the functional

days after a parade, especially the Twelfth of July parade, the music would resound in my head and the icons on the banners would flow across the screen of my mind. At band practice one night it was casually announced that it was my time to join the Order, so I showed up as expected at the Orange Hall.

The initiation was a hair-raising experience. I arrived in good time for the meeting and was ushered into the ante-room where the tea was prepared for later consumption. I was stripped to my waist; my socks and shoes were removed. My trousers were rolled up to my knees. I was carefully blindfolded before being led into the main room in fear and trembling. There was a deathly silence. Suddenly, I heard a sound like the sound of single shot from a gun. I nearly jumped out of my skin. The blindfold was removed; I could see that the sound came from the impact of a leather belt that had been brought down forcefully upon a wooden table by one of the more muscular members. The next step was the administering of the oath. I was led across the blazing fireplace to stand before an old man who proceeded to recite a narrative of such length that I have no idea how he managed to learn it and recite it completely from memory. I was so impressed with the rhetoric and the verbal feat that I have no idea what was said. I do recall the end of it. He looked me straight in the eye and insisted that if ever I divulged anything that went on in the meetings then my tongue should be cut out of my mouth, sliced up into little pieces, and scattered to the four winds to be devoured by the fowls of the air. That said, I was blindfolded once more and then led on a symbolic tour around the hall, crisscrossing it from one side to the other to make maximum use of the space. The floor was covered in places with sand, rocks, twigs, and thorns. At intervals the little marching party halted for readings from the Old Testament. It was clear that we were reenacting the journey of Israel out of Egypt through the desert and on to the Promised Land.

We then got to the climax of the evening. Still blindfolded, I was led up the stairs and on to the stage at the other end of the hall. With great precision I was turned around and stood up in such a way that my heels were jutting out over the end of the stage. It was a precarious stance, for at any moment I could have tumbled backwards and fallen hard onto the floor below the stage. Before I

---

equivalent of the Fourth of July in the USA.

had time to worry about this, I was unceremoniously shoved off the stage into mid-air. As I flew into empty space I could hear noises that resembled the bleating and baying of goats. I actually thought that there were real goats in the hall and that they had been coached to break forth in bleating once I was launched from the stage. I had picked up beforehand by rumor and innuendo that I would get to ride the goat; so this, I thought, was were the goats had been summoned. Expecting the worst, that is, that I would come crashing to the floor and be injured, I was caught in a sheet and tumbled up and down with great gusto by those who were holding various ends of it. When the blindfold was removed, I could see that there were no goats. The baying and bleating had come from the members who were having the time of their lives scaring the living daylights out of me.

I have no idea how this form of initiation had been worked out and developed. It clearly involved a network of rituals that bonded the members together. It neatly folded the birth of British ethnic identity into the story of the liberation of Israel from Egypt. When I studied various forms of liberation theology later I already knew the basic grammar of the move to root politics in stories of bondage and release. In this instance the language of liberation was reiterated in terms that emphasized freedom of conscience and religion, noting the critical role of Protestantism in birthing the modern political experience of progress and liberty. The point of the initiation was to weld together the biblical narrative of redemption with the British political values of Northern Ireland. The process as a whole was a mixture of recital, drama, role-playing, and mild instruction. The process ended in a humorous bout of rough play that scared the life out of me at the time but was totally harmless in its effect.

This sense of harmlessness remained with me all the time I was a member. The meetings were perfunctory and were taken up with deciding what was to be done at the next meeting. Ever since then I have detested badly run committee meetings that cannot get down to business. The big events of the year were the Twelfth of July celebrations, the Christmas dinner, and the occasional bazaar to raise money. I recall with some satisfaction winning a splendid rooster that made a fine Sunday lunch; I accidentally managed to hit the best score of the evening at the dartboard.

I resigned from the Order on theological grounds when I was

a doctoral student in philosophy at Oxford; I simply rejected its vision of Catholicism; besides, I had never bought the Orange Order's ideas on the relationship between the Christian gospel and politics. Yet I had to seek out the theological vision at the heart of the Orange Order for myself. Nobody took the trouble to explain it to me. The Order was hopelessly ineffective in handing over its teaching; perhaps forgetting the Protestant bias against rituals, its members hoped that ritual alone would suffice. In fact there was no substance to the Order beyond the celebration of the victory of King William over King James at the Battle of the Boyne in 1690. The whole experience taught me that the Orange Order was a toothless tiger. Once when I was traveling alone in a Catholic area near Coa, where my maternal grandparents lived, I was stopped by a group of tough young men who accused me of being an Orange bastard. From their gestures and tone this was clearly a very bad thing to be; they looked at me as if I was a demon from within the bowels of Protestantism. In reality Orangemen were decent ordinary people who found in the Order a fraternal, social organization where class boundaries disappeared and where they could publicly express their political ideals with symbolic and musical flair.

My personal experience, of course, is one thing; the public face and practice of the Orange Order is another. Orange men are not allowed to marry Roman Catholics; if they do, they are expelled; the agony at that point can run deep. Nor are they permitted to attend Roman Catholic services; happily affection for neighbors undermined this rule and members do attend the funerals of their friends from the other side. I enjoyed visiting Roman Catholic churches and was fascinated by the iconography; I also was on the lookout for the tracts to be found in the vestibule on entry. A robust form of Protestant theology is still enacted as the prevailing background music within the Orange Order. When the Order divided in 1903, it split over that background music. The founders of the new Independent Loyal Orange Order wanted to stay clear of party politics and stick to the great slogans of the Reformation: Scripture alone, Christ alone, grace alone, and faith alone. However, this is a purely intramural dispute. In both Orders, the old and the new, the political commitments are primary. The real purpose of the mainstream Orange Order is to be a carrier of Ulster British identity and a means of getting out the vote. Even then, there are limits to its appeal. Many of my friends from my student days were astonished at my participation; they saw the Order as part of the comedy of Northern Irish culture and as a distraction from the real issues in politics. The exceptions here prove the rule. The politics of Ulster drew on the oxygen of the Protestant faith explicitly and publicly. Supplying oxygen for local politics was the primary purpose of the Orange Order.

It is, however, very easy to present a sinister vision of the Orange Order and of Northern Irish politics. Take the version of Father Sean McManus. Father McManus comes from the village of Kinawley not far from Enniskillen. Kinawley has two shops, a pub, a post office, a credit union, and seventy-five inhabitants. Father McManus has made it to the big-time as President of the Irish National Caucus in Washington D.C.. From his own experience in and around Kinawley he is aware that there are many decent, fair-minded Protestants in the Orange Order. His take on the Orange Order is illuminating. On the surface the Orange Order is the personification of anti-Catholic bigotry; it exists to promote and protect the Protestant domination over Catholics in Ireland. Beneath the surface, however, he thinks that there is a more sinister agency at work. The Order is really a tool of British imperialism. The real issue is one of empire, race, and economics. Behind the Orange Order is a supremacist ideology; it is the white-collar version of the Klu Klux Klan, invented to dupe more respectable and moderate people. For Father McManus the Orange Order is an imperial organization with a religious facade. Thus he gleefully notes that the British Act of Settlement of 1701, much beloved by Orangemen, does not allow a Catholic or anyone married to a Catholic to sit on the British throne and absolves any allegiance to them. There are rumbles about this at present in Britain for Prince Charles wants to find a way to be inclusive of all religions; so the debate about this is not over.

No doubt there are Orange leaders for whom the prohibitions on Catholics on the British throne is a matter of nervous rejoicing. But they do not share Father McManus' reading of their traditions. On the one hand, the British Empire is now dead; on this score Father McManus's claims are complete fantasy. On the other hand, many Orangemen suspect that Britain would love to disengage from Northern Ireland as its first and last colonial outpost.

British officialdom long ago figured out that the best way to tackle the problem of Northern Ireland was the same as elsewhere in the empire: withdraw as quickly and quietly as possible. Orangemen do not trust the British in London as far as they could throw them; they constantly worry about plants inside their leadership who will betray them; and they see British civil servants as allied to the cause of Irish unity and nationalism. What matters to Orangemen is that they keep their Ulster British identity, their Protestant culture, their democratic traditions, and their place inside the United Kingdom. In fact, outside the noble personage of Queen Elizabeth, they think that the current Royal family is a moral and religious embarrassment that should be passed over in silence.

Sorting Out the Issues in Ireland

What light does all this throw on the relation between religion and terrorism? Was my initial intuition that they are radically distinct and separate correct? Or does the connection between religion and politics in Ireland reveal a more complex interpretation of the relation?

It is patently clear that there is no conceptual relation between religion and terrorism. There is nothing in the logic or meaning of religion that would imply terrorism; and there is nothing in the logic and meaning of terrorism that would require religion.

We can go further when we look specifically at the Christian religion in Ireland. There is no material relation between religion and terrorism either. There was and is no divine command to go out and slay heretics or to kill the enemy. In fact, the mandates go the other way: the New Testament commands us to love our enemies. The Old Testament texts that sanctioned holy war were at this point clearly presented as superseded and abrogated by the New Testament. Indeed I have always been fascinated by John Wesley's comment that passages in the Psalms that expressed violence towards the enemy were not fit for the mouth of a Christian congregation. This rattles people when I mention it, but they get the point that the religious texts of the bible are set in a wider context of interpretation and reception. This important observation is now beginning to crop up in debates about the meaning of Islam.

It was equally clear, of course, that the Christian religion to which I was exposed allowed for violence in cases of defensive war. So lethal force was permitted, but the use of force emphatically did not extend as far as terrorism. Christian faith set constraints on the use of force and undermined every effort to glory in violence or to kill innocent people for political purposes. Thus the Christian religion did not rule out the use of force, but it emphatically ruled out terrorism. War was brought inside the tent and tamed and tempered. This was the moral air I breathed. The presence of Quakers raised the possibility of pacifism, but it was a minority report that I found interesting but unconvincing. I tried once in a youth group meeting to defend pacifism rigorously, but it fell apart on me in my own exposition. The default position then was a tacit approval of just war theory. To be sure, various leaders flirted with forms of pavement politics in which they would take to the streets to protest, to challenge state policy and action, and galvanize their supporters. But this is now commonplace in our social life, and it is a long way from terrorism. Terrorism was not a moral option; it was universally rejected.[10]

This judgment is borne out by the terrorists on the so-called Loyalist side of the aisle. They took up terrorism and then did what they could to house it within a theory of self-defense. They offered no serious theological rationale for their practices. Nor could they find one in the Orange Order, for even the Orange Order did not tamper with the clear teaching of the Christian faith. In fact, it was well known that there were two ways out of loyalist terrorism: either feet-first in a coffin or by being born again in a religious conversion. In the first option you could be shot either by the opposition as an enemy or by your colleagues as a traitor; in the second you could find God and your comrades would give you a free exit pass. In the latter case we see what they believed. They were well aware that the believer would in conscience want to get out of terrorism; and they had sufficient fear of God not to mess with his followers; so they were prepared to let them go despite the loss of valuable personnel. Overall, loyalist terrorists saw themselves as Ulster nationalists ready to defend their British identity and to answer in kind the terrorism they saw emanating from nationalist circles.[11] This was a

[10]For ample documentation see Steve Bruce, "Religion and Violence: The Case of Paisley and Ulster Evangelicals," in Dennis Kennedy, ed., *Nothing but Trouble? Religion and the Irish Problem* (Belfast: Irish Association for Cultural, Economic and Social Relations, 2004), 30–44.

[11]One exception to this is the case of Billy Wright, a terrorist in a loyalist splinter group, the LVF (Loyalist Volunteer Force), who was killed by the INLA (Irish Na-

sufficient justification, if they needed one. They did not look to faith for warrant or inspiration.

The same judgment holds initially for the main nationalist terrorist group, the IRA. Their first and last commitment is political, that is, to the reunification of Ireland. As they see it, Ireland has four green fields. Three have gained their independence; the fourth needs to be added to them. The way to get there was by a combination of the Armalite rifle and the ballot box, although how far the latter matters was up for discussion until very recently. The rest is customizing the costume. So the terrorist case can be decked out in stories of imperialism, colonialism, racism, bigotry, oppression, class warfare, and discrimination.

The upshot to this point is that there is no direct relation between religion and terrorism in Ireland. Yet there is an indirect and important connection. The crux of the matter is simple: terrorists in Ireland are adept at using the resources and debris of religion when it suits them for their own nefarious ends.

Interestingly this observation applies more on the nationalist side than it does on the loyalist side. Loyalist terrorists may speak of being Protestants, but 'Protestant' for them is an ethnic and not a religious designation. More vaguely, 'Protestant' may be a placeholder for a cluster of political values like liberty of conscience, freedom of religion, equality, and democracy. Thus it is common in Northern Ireland to claim that one is a Protestant but not a Christian. 'Protestant' could mean 'not Catholic'; it often meant 'not Christian'. This was exactly how I saw myself in my childhood. To be Protestant in the religious sense was to be 'good-living', an expression that alerted the perceptive listener to the fact that religion for the Protestant was cast in a certain vision of the inward, moral, and spiritual, rather than in a vision that was sacramental, liturgical, and external. On these terms it was simply impossible to recast the terrorist commitments in terms of religion.

There is one possible exception to this judgment that I can identify. Jim McDonald, a member of the Orange Order in Belfast, developed it nicely in an interview on October 23, 1972 that showed

---

tional Liberation Army) in 1997. Wright proves how Irish he was in noting that he believed the gospel and because of that he believed he would be damned by God for his terrorist activity. See Chris Anderson, *The Billy Boy: The Life and Death of LVF Leader Billy Wright* (Belfast: Mainstream Publishing, 2002).

up in *Chicago Today*.[12] McDonald insisted that there was a global war between Catholicism and communism. He was convinced that the Catholic strategy involved a very special place for Ireland. Given that the pope feared that communists would take over Italy, he intended to use a united Catholic Ireland as a base to launch a counter-offensive to defeat communism and to give the Catholic Church world domination. So wonderful little Northern Irish Protestantism, led by banners, bands, an orange lily, and a big drum has a lead role in saving the world from Rome rule. It is hard to know where Jim McDonald got this nonsense; he probably invented it on the spot, for there are very few sources from which to mine it. What he might be drawing on is a vague conspiratorial sense that Rome is out to rule the world and that her sights are firmly set on destroying the last bastion of true religion in the entire world, that is, in Northern Ireland. This is an ancient song in various parts of the West. One can find something akin to it in Ian Paisley at times, but very few believe it, for this kind of pious mythology is not even shared by many of McDonald's fellow Orangemen. They would find its recital the occasion for a good laugh.

Terrorism on the nationalist side, given its Catholic background music, has had an easier run at exploiting the resources of religion. For starters, there was a mythic history to draw on. The story of Ireland was cast in terms of a grand narrative of creation, fall, and redemption. In its initial creation Ireland was a land of peace and glory, of perfect, pure religion and people; then there was a fall when the demonic forces of British imperialism invaded and ruined everything; but redemption had arrived with national independence; we are now in the birth pangs of the great and final day of redemption when all her people will be set free.

Within this grand narrative the story of Irish independence in the early twentieth century was presented as a narrative of sacrifice and resurrection. Mother Ireland had offered up her sons in a sacrifice of blood; the next step was an Easter Rising to New Life. It was certainly not accidental that the Irish rebels in 1916 exploited this imagery in choosing the Easter weekend as their time to strike. When they died they were recast as saints, forming a mystical canon with their own songs, days of commemoration, and written

[12]See Lawrence J. McCaffrey, "Irish Nationalism and Irish Catholicism: A Study in Cultural Identity," *Church History*, 42 (1973), 530.

icons. To follow their inspiration was to come to a new baptism and to enter into a new regeneration and cleansing. To take up their message and spread it abroad was to embrace a new gospel. Even their graves become holy places, more sacred than that of St. Patrick in Downpatrick. Any and every departure from these practices was a form of heresy. Embracing them was a form of conspicuous sanctity.

Turning Thugs into Saints

Nowhere is this more visible than in the death of Bobby Sands, who became the Member of Parliament for the Enniskillen area after the death of the sitting MP, Frank Maguire, in 1981. At the time of his election Sands was serving a prison service for possession of firearms with intent to endanger life. He was also the leader of a group of hunger strikers who were determined to regain their status as political prisoners rather than as common criminals. Refusing to wear prison uniforms on the grounds that they were political prisoners, Sands and his colleagues went naked, wearing only the blanket from their beds. When this brought about the natural reaction from the prison authorities a spiral of malevolence set in. Denied tobacco, wives and friends smuggled it in up their anal passage in hollow ballpoint pens. One enterprising chap brought in three pencils and another hid a pen, a comb, and lighter. As a result bleeding was inevitable; sometimes pieces of flesh came off. Refusing to leave their cells the blanket men then refused to empty their chamber pots. Pots overflowed; windows were smashed; metal grills were installed; excrement was spread on the walls with foam culled from the mattresses; maggots multiplied on the ensuing feast; diarrhea only added to the filth and stench. The prisoners refused to wash, shave, or have their hair cut. After three years of protest, a determined core group finally went on hunger strike.

Sands' election was part of a wider campaign to embarrass the government and force concessions. He was elected on 9 April 1981, with 30,493 votes over his opponent who got 29,046 votes. Three weeks later, on May 5, aged 27, he died of starvation after 66 days on hunger strike. In the aftermath Sands became a martyr and hero. Between 80,000 and 100,000 attended his funeral. Gerry Adams solemnly called on the crowd not to desecrate the day by getting into a confrontation with the security forces. Over 1,000 people gathered in New York's St. Patrick's Cathedral where Cardinal Cook offered a Mass of reconciliation for Northern Ireland. Irish bars in the city were closed for two hours in mourning. Sands was lauded in Milan, Ghent, Oslo, and Hong Kong. Street names were changed to Sands in Nantes, Le Mans, St. Denis in France, and in Tehran in Iran. Monuments were unveiled in Hartford, Connecticut and in Havana, Cuba. At least fourteen songs were written in response to his death. A film about him, *Some Mother's Son*, was released in 1996.

Bobby Sands was not content to see himself as merely a secular, nationalist hero. On receiving his fourteen-year sentence, he wrote:

> The beady eyes they peered at me
> The time had come to be,
> To walk the lonely road
> Like that of Calvary.
> *And take up the cross of Irishmen*
> Who've carried liberty.

The self-portrait was not missed in a book written to further the cause Sands represented. John Feehan solemnly tells us that on his last birthday, "He (Sands) was thrilled to get a picture of our Lady from a priest in Kerry who had encouraged him to take up arms for his oppressed people."[13] When Cardinal Hume made it clear that men like Sands, by deliberately starving themselves to death, were committing suicide, Feehan replied: "Jesus Christ could have saved his life when he came before Pilate but he refused to do so. Did the founder of Christianity therefore commit suicide?"[14] Feehan gets bolder in his comparison between Sands and Jesus. "In the quiet evening silence of Milltown graveyard it seemed as if the Republican Movement had reached its Calvary with no Resurrection in sight, that Bobby Sands had lost and the overwhelming power of the British Empire had won yet another victory."[15] The boost given to the Republican cause by the death of the hunger strikes did proxy for the resurrection. Feehan is not finished with Sands just yet; his death is a very special one. "In the early hours of the morning of 5 May the immortal soul of one of the noblest young Irishmen of the twentieth century came face to face with his Fellow-Sufferer and

[13] Quoted in Conor Cruise O'Brien, *Passion and Cunning and Other Essays* (New York: Simon and Shuster, 1988), 204.
[14] Ibid., 203.
[15] Ibid.

Maker. Bobby Sands was dead."[16] Clearly Sands was well on his way
to being elevated to the status of Jesus Christ, his Fellow-Sufferer.
Sand's place in the canon of saints was now secure; hagiography had
a new martyr to commemorate.[17]

It is not known with certainty if that hagiography mentions the
tobacco that was neatly packed in hollow ballpoint pens and insert-
ed up the anal passage of visitors. It is a tad difficult to figure out the
spiritual significance of such heroism and generosity. Maybe one of
those skinheads from Germany who have turned Mad Dog Johnny
Adair into a hero will be able to work this out for our children and
our children's children. Maybe one of those icon painters in Belfast
will be able to work it into one of the paintings on the gable walls
and turn it into a glorious tourist attraction that will inspire future
generations to conspicuous sanctity.

None of this process of canonization is possible for loyalist terrorists who died in the cause of Ulster-British nationalism. The best
their friends can muster is a little porridge bowl of mythic history
in which Catholicism is set upon by communism and needs a united Ireland to launch a counter-offensive. The religious background
music has been gutted of the concepts and practices that make this
kind of makeover possible. For Ulster loyalists there is no canon
of saints. Salvation is a more ethereal affair; it would be blasphemy
to link it to nationalism. The suffering they endure is an entirely
human affair; it cannot be mentioned in the same breath as the suffering of Jesus Christ.

We can now see the connection between religion and terrorism
in Ireland. Religious themes and practices are readily picked up and
deployed to lend depth and warrant to terrorist acts and agents.
Terrorists are very public agents; when they blow up the public
square they need inner resources; they need ideas and themes to
cover up the blood they have spilt. No doubt many can murder and
maim without any outside help; they welcome the drama, the secrecy, and the thrill of killing. But ordinary people are repelled and
disgusted; and terrorists have to live among them. Thus they gladly
reach for resources of self-deception and public delusion. Cultural
and religious debris that they can use at this point are readily at

[16] Ibid.

[17] This whole way of thinking runs deep in the mythology of Irish nationalism. For
a devastating and courageous review see Francis Shaw, S. J. "The Canon of Irish
History—A Challenge," *Studies* 61 (Summer 1972), 113–153.

hand in Ireland. It is easy to pick up the rotted and dry remains of a religious heritage that has been entwined with ethnicity and nationalism over centuries. Indeed such material is intrinsically combustible, for it was originally the carrier of light and life. Transposed into secular idiom it can burn and serve as kindling for the fires of violence.

In the nationalist case there is much more debris to exploit. Catholicism and Irish nationalism have been deeply intertwined for centuries. The Catholic Church has kept alive older elements of the Christian faith that can readily be turned inside out and used for political purposes. The narrative of creation, fall, and redemption is constantly reiterated and thus stands ready to be filled with false meaning. There are saints and icons to be transposed and substituted with new faces. In the loyalist case there is less debris lying around, for the resources are thin; the whole bent of the tradition is toward inward transformation. Even the exotic inventions of the Orange Order are sufficiently clear to make the commitment to terrorism obviously evil. So loyalists have to reach for a purely ethnic vision of Protestantism and of the Orange Order if they are to turn there for moral and intellectual support. Fortunately, in both instances we can see through the façade to the abuse involved.

Reclaiming the Treasures of the Faith

The good news in all this is that we can genuinely deploy the resources of the Christian faith in order to tackle the challenge of terrorism. We can begin by gathering up the debris and disposing of it. Once we know where religious themes and practices are being abused we can intervene and challenge such usage at its foundations. We can mount a sharp critique upon terrorism that appeals to the canonical faith of the church without apology. We can also issue sharp warnings about our own mistakes across the centuries when violence was used for religious purposes or when religion was used inappropriately for political purposes. And we can redirect the oxygen and energy of religion to confront terrorism and to find ways to contain or eradicate it. Ironically, the massive losses in nominal Christian faith and practice have cleared the decks for a retrieval of common Christian materials and practices.

I am not saying that other resources are not crucial. Nor should it surprise or depress us that we need to deal with terrorism from a host of angles. If terrorism in Ireland has been taken up in order to further the cause of Irish or British nationalism, then we know what kind of solutions to pursue. We need a combination of philosophical, cultural, political, economic, and military measures. Of course, sorting out what all this means in practice is a hit and miss affair. We should expect that there will inevitably be false starts and dead ends. Perhaps all we may hope for in a lifetime is to contain terrorism, to begin the mainstreaming of its agents, to deprive it of intellectual oxygen, and to move towards more rational ways of resolving those social and political disputes that readily spill over into violence.

We can readily summarize the factors that have combined to bring about change in Ireland. Effective military action has convinced the terrorists that they cannot achieve their ends. The Republic of Ireland has halted its harboring of terrorists. The United States of America has awakened to the danger of terrorism and has taken a second look at its role in Ireland. 9/11 has undercut much of the financial and political support for the IRA; it has also undercut the moral illusions that lay behind that support. Revisionist historians are undermining the historical myths and legends that have been passed off as true and illuminating. The police force was renamed, given a smart new uniform, and radically restructured. Cultural innovators are finding ways to turn the colorful gatherings of the Orange Order into folk festivals and tourist attractions.[18] The site of the Battle of the Boyne is earmarked to become a theme park. The cultural innovators have also made it possible for alienated groups to own St. Patrick as a model of faith and as a cultural treasure. In the St. Patrick tourist center in Downpatrick there is a stunning three-dimensional movie in which all sides (including Ian Paisley) talk in glowing terms about his legacy. For their part politicians have fought it out inch-by-inch, clause-by-clause, and insult-by-insult, to find structures and institutions that will bring everybody to the table. Leaders across the community have broken loose from unhealthy taboos and restrictive practices. Ordinary citizens have patiently voted; and they have held their noses as they have dealt with the messy morality of prisoner release. Clergy and priests have done what they can to keep hope alive. Extraordinary

---

[18] For an account of how this has happened to the celebration of Guy Fawkes Night in England, see Colm Tóibín, *The Sign of the Cross: Travels in Catholic Europe* (London: J. Cape, 1994), 250–3.

commercial success has opened up more creative and fruitful ways of living that wean folk off the addiction to violence.

It was a great day for all the Irish for the moment. Irish eyes were smiling. Then some militant Muslims started attacking innocent civilians across the world. We are right back where we started.

3
—

In the Name of God

The Transition to New York

We leave the rainy, green fields of Ireland and shift to the sunny, windy shores of New York.

On the night before 9/11 nineteen Islamist terrorists affiliated with al-Qaeda began their preparations for their work the next day.[19] They had done all the standard kind of things that terrorists have to do to get ready for a murderous operation. They had gone through rigorous training and indoctrination. They had selected their targets, worked out the details of the impending operation with precision, and gone over the final minutiae together. Now they were down to the very the last items. They checked their ID's, passports, and papers. They removed excess hair from their bodies, took a shower, and sprayed themselves with perfume. They examined their bags and their clothes, especially their socks and shoes. They checked their weapons, making sure that their knives were properly sharpened. They steeled their mind once more, knowing that they would have to tame their emotions, be patient in meeting resistance, and be disciplined in listening and obeying. They searched their hearts, ridding them of all worldly ambitions. In and through all these preparations they drew on the manifold resources of their faith. The preparation and practice on this score were de-

[19]The graphic details can be found in "September 11: The Letter Left Behind," in Walter Laqueur, *Voices of Terror* (New York: Reed Press, 2004), 413–419.

tailed and comprehensive.

Prayer accompanied every step. They asked God for victory, first in the middle of the night and many times thereafter. They prayed for forgiveness for their sins and for any extravagance in their work to date. The latter perhaps included forgiveness for attendance at strip clubs, no doubt a strategy to deter detection if not a means of anticipating future sensual bliss. As they went to work, they prayed for the overpowering of the enemy, for facilitation of the operation, for protective covering, for their souls, for the knives, for the details of the taxi journey to go expeditiously, for blindness on the part of airport personnel, for patience, and for peace on entering the aircraft. They asked for firmness as they clenched their teeth in battle, for God to be present with them in the cutting of throats, and for help in opening their jackets and chests to welcome death. They also requested the ability to smile through it all.

They read and pondered crucial chapters of the Qur'an. They reviewed the chapters on "The Spoils of War" and "Repentance of the Holy Qur'an." They recalled that God had said that they should not dispute among themselves, and that many small groups can defeat a big one if God permits. They noted again that God was mightier than all His creation, that the devil makes his agents afraid, that they should hit their adversaries on the necks and on every finger, and that there should be no prisoners of war until the enemy is weakened. Above all they recalled that there is no God but Allah. Thus they immersed themselves in the true and final revelation that God had given to the world. It was salutary and sufficient to rely on the Word of the Lord.

They remembered and savored relevant doctrines at the heart of Islam. God is the God of all creation, so He had created them for a purpose, and they can depend on Him. Angels were there to guard them and make supplication for them. God is a God of providence. He can make a dam for them before their fronts and their backs; no devices, doors, or technology have any benefit in slaughter unless He permits it; He can weaken the tricks of the disbelievers. God is a God of grace and salvation. Those who say that there is no God but Allah, believing it with all their heart, enter paradise. They will pass through the Judgment, and the most beautiful women in paradise will receive them. Paradise has already been prepared with the best of its decorations and ornaments; the most beautiful women already call them to come, so they dress in their best attire for them.

The whole world knows what happened next. The terrorists took over four commercial aircraft and used them as flying bombs, most dramatically in the case of the World Trade Center Towers in New York City. Each of the jet airliners had a fuel capacity of 24,000 US gallons. By the time it was all over the nineteen hijackers along with 2,973 people were dead; another 24 were missing and presumed dead. Hundreds were killed instantly; 200 jumped to their death from burning towers; 400 rescue workers died when buildings collapsed on top of them. Those who died came from no less than 62 different countries, including 250 from India, 200 from Pakistan, 200 from Britain, 55 from Australia, and 23 from Japan. There was among them a Barbie Doll collector, a Palestinian accountant, an ex-hippie stockbroker, a Japanese Hockey player, a vegetarian calligrapher, and an Ecuadoran sous chef. The number who died was comparable to the total number who had died in Northern Ireland since the 1970s. It was 600 more than the number at Pearl Harbor on December 7, 1941 and thirty times greater than the number killed in the Oklahoma City bombing on April 19, 1995.

It is not easy to make the shift from Enniskillen to New York. This is true when we think of the numbers killed, the damage done, the cost of rebuilding, and the global consequences. It is equally true when we try to make the shift intellectually. Terrorist groups are like snowflakes. From a distance they look the same; up close they are radically different. Of course, for the victims and their relatives, these differences are cold comfort, for the impact is the same. The victims have been killed or injured; the relatives are left to mourn and work through their grief. In meeting with relatives of policemen killed in Armagh, for example, I have seen the grief of mothers and fathers written in their faces and traceable in their voices close to twenty years after the fateful days when their children were killed. However, terrorist acts are as specific as the causes they represent, the personalities that perform them, the motives that drive them, and the contexts in which they take place. This is why it helps to stay close to the ground and work through the questions that bother us case-by-case, comparison-by-comparison, and disanology-by-disanalogy. Nowhere is this truer than when we try to understand the relation between religion and terrorism.

The Transition to Theology

We can see immediately that religion and terrorism are intimately connected in the case of al-Qaeda in a way that is radically different from the Irish situation. It is not just that there are no records of Irish terrorists that display the religious commitment and sensibility clearly on display in the case of the 9/11 terrorists. The truth is that if we were to find them, we would dismiss them as fabrications. They would be surreal, given what we know of modern Christianity in Ireland. The best terrorists can do in Ireland is to go on a clever fishing expedition in murky waters in the hopes of catching a fish or two that can be cooked and garnished to suit their purposes. Their primary commitments are nationalist and political rather than religious and theological. So they cannot and do not appeal in any serious way to the core of the Christian tradition, that is, to the teaching and practice of its founder, to its clear moral imperatives, or to its primary doctrines. Not even the colorful waters of the Orange Order or the virulent form of Political Protestantism invented by the Rev. Dr. Ian Paisley will yield up a slithery, silver minnow. Nor will any canonical version of Catholicism, a tradition that has very explicit ways of identifying its official teaching, yield an endorsement for terrorism.

The situation that confronts us in the case of al-Qaeda, though, is quite different. The terrorists of 9/11 infamy were not driven by secular nationalism but by religious faith. They exhibited conspicuous piety; they were steeped in the Qur'an; they drew on central doctrines of their religion. Their faith was not superficial but substantial, not merely formal but utterly sincere, not episodic but consistent and deep. We have entered into a whole new world where religion is directly related to terrorism. The evidence already in hand is conclusive: in the case of 9/11 we encounter terrorism that is rooted in theology and in robust religious practices. Yet the stakes are so high it is important to go the extra mile and see if this conclusion can be sustained. We are not interested in polemics and partisan criticism; we are looking for the sober truth.

We start from what we know. First, al-Qaeda, led by Osama bin Laden, was deeply involved in the terrorist attack of 9/11. Initially bin Laden distanced himself, limiting his comments to endorsement and praise; but in time he acknowledged his role and responsibility. So 9/11 was not, as some North American theologians have fantasized, a cleverly orchestrated event masterminded by American political leaders in order to go to war or to further their imperialist ambitions. Theologians who live in an unreal theological lalaland dreamed up in their speculative imaginations have a tendency to invent their own fantasy world of events when it comes to the real world. Second, al-Qaeda lays claim to be based on an authentic interpretation of Islam. In fact, it can draw on a fascinating version of Islam that has clear affinities with forms of Protestantism in its appeal to an original and pure version of the earliest traditions. Here, we are dealing with a sincere, industrial strength version of religious faith. Third, al-Qaeda does not hesitate to kill innocent civilians for political purposes, and thus it fits our working account of terrorism. Hence in the case of al-Qaeda we cannot fudge on the relation between religion and terrorism. In personal relations with others and in our political speech it is important at times to hold our tongues and soften our speech, but there is a time when only straight talk will capture what is at stake in dealing with terrorism. With al-Qaeda we have a serious religious group engaging in horrendous acts of terrorism.

Everything hinges at this point on how we interpret the relation between terrorism and Islam. There are two issues here. The first is this: Is the terrorism of al-Qaeda motivated and warranted by an authentic vision of Islam? Are we dealing in this instance with a true form of Islam committed to terrorism or are we dealing with Muslims who just happen also to be terrorists? Do we encounter a valid form of Islam or do we encounter terrorists dressed out in the costume of Islam, used illegitimately as a mechanism of rhetoric and self-deception? The second issue is this: If we are dealing with a genuine vision of Islam, is this vision of Islam representative of Islam or is it a fringe version of Islam? Is it mainstream or is it unconventional? Is it the majority report or is it a minority report?

Let's begin with the issue of the relation between terrorism and Islam.

There is no question that bin Laden and his cohorts were committed to killing innocent civilians as a religious duty. The fatwā they issued on 23 February, 1998, makes this clear.

> The ruling to kill the Americans and their allies—civilians and military—is an individual duty for every Muslim who can do it in any country in which it is possible to do so, in order to liberate the al-Aqsa mosque and the holy mosque [Mecca] from their

grip, and in order for their armies to move out of all lands of Islam, defeated and unable to threaten any Muslim. This is in accordance with the word of Almighty Allah, "and fight the pagans all together as they fight you all together," and "fight until there is no more tumult or oppression, and there prevail justice and faith in Allah."[20]

This proclamation was not a generic call to arms, and it was more than the appeal to the slippery concept of jihad. It was a legal pronouncement intended to settle a question where Islamic jurisprudence is unclear. Moreover, it fulfilled the conventional rules for a fatwā. It was in line with relevant legal proofs derived from the Qur'an and hadith; it was issued by those who have appropriate knowledge and sincerity of heart; it was free from individual opportunism and not dependent on political servitude; and it was relative to the needs of the contemporary world.

It is tempting to cavil at the details here by questioning the basis of the ruling in the Qur'an and hadith, by challenging the sincerity and knowledge base of those who issued it, and so on, all down the line. All this is possible, but it is beside the point. We can contest every single item in the list of conditions; but this is the case with virtually every fatwā. There are no problem-free readings of the relevant texts and circumstances, and there never have been. If we insist on uncontested interpretations we are setting up conditions of success that are unreal, that would undermine the legitimacy of a host of fatwās. Such standards are therefore irrelevant. Fatwās arise precisely because there is a question of law where Islamic jurisprudence is unclear. We can assume that they will generate further discussion and interpretation; they do not eliminate debate. Their chief function is to provide religious and moral legitimacy in a religion that recognizes law as a regulator of all life. The fatwās should not be dismissed as religious terminology cynically deployed as religious propaganda.

Nor can we evade the status of this fatwā by claiming that there is no official way to decide the authenticity of a fatwā within Islam. There is no *magisterium* in Islam as found in Roman Catholicism, where there is a relatively clear-cut way to identify and interpret official matters of faith and practice. If we are unsure of what this or that ruling means, we can turn to the official teachers of the church and get help in sorting out what is involved. Even then, papal pro-

[20]Laqueur, *Voices of Terror*, 412.

nouncements can be elusive; but we can be sure that there will be a follow-up pronouncement from the Pope to set us straight. However, the appeal to the practices of Roman Catholicism is a red herring. Islam has never had such a mechanism and has no desire to develop one. In this respect Islam is much more akin to the sprawling, chaotic world of Protestantism where there is no centralized authority and little or no impetus to create one. The conditions for determining an authentic fatwā are imprecise and contested; so a fatwā does not have to meet this alien standard to be valid. It is not even enough to point out that one fatwā may contradict another fatwā, as often happens when there is no official, centralized organ of endorsement. We can, in fact, only have a contradiction between fatwās if we have two fatwās in hand; otherwise we only have a contradiction between a fatwā and some other sort of pronouncement. So the fatwā in question falls well within the boundaries of a genuine fatwā.

There are plenty of reasons for accepting, moreover, that this is a very significant fatwā. We are not dealing here with a minor ruling that can be dismissed as obscure and accidental. Four reasons will suffice to establish this judgment.

First, the source is secure. The fatwā in question was issued by the hand of Osama bin Laden, a man considered a hero within much of the worldwide Muslim community. Bin Laden was a devout Muslim whose faith was sincere and entirely consonant with the general practices of Sunni Islam. Indeed for some he was the paradigm of the good Muslim, gladly abandoning a life of luxury and wealth to serve the cause of Islam. He conspicuously exhibited the Muslim virtues of moral outrage, self-sacrifice, otherworldliness, and brotherhood. His piety was exemplary.

Second, the reception of the fatwā is secure. Bin Laden had won the affection and allegiance of many Muslims across the world and they were glad to accept his rulings. Mothers named their children after him; his face was an icon of true piety; his videos and writings commanded avid attention. Most importantly, he was able to recruit an army of fighters in his own militant organization who were more than ready to take him as their teacher and leader. Beyond that he was a source of inspiration and hope for many ordinary Muslims and for a host of militant Muslim terrorist groups.

Third, the fatwā fits with a serious reading of the Islamic traditions. Bin Laden could legitimately appeal to a deep resonance with elements in the Islamic tradition that have been brilliantly worked out across the centuries. They have continuities with Ibn Taymiyyah's (1263–1328) call to armed resistance in the twelfth century, with the Wahabbi tradition in Saudi Arabia in the eighteenth century, with the Indian thinker, Abu Ala Maududi (1903–1979), and with the Egyptian theologian Sayed Qutb (1906–1966). Bin Laden can take his place in a long tradition of Islamic liberation theology that looks to the earliest traditions of Islam as the norm of faith and practice. He was not an isolated aberration crying in the wilderness on his own.

Fourth, the fatwā can without undue awkwardness be placed within a narrative of Islamic history that is persuasive and not just exploitative. It coheres nicely with a vision of Islam committed to recapturing Muslim homelands, ridding the Islamic holy sites of foreign troops, eliminating Israel, restoring the Caliphate, and spreading the truth of Islam as a religious and political ideology across the world. If it does not exactly fit with the idea of jihad or holy warfare, it can do so with minimum extension.

It is no surprise to find that bin Laden appealed to the practice of jihad to underwrite terrorist acts. As he saw it, the presence of American troops in the holiest of places, the massacres of Iraqis in the first Gulf war and its aftermath, and the support of the "Jews' petty state" constituted "a clear declaration of war on Allah, his Messenger, and Muslims." "...ulema have throughout the Islamic history unanimously agreed that jihad is an individual duty if the enemy destroys the Muslim countries."[21] Hence bin Laden carefully grounded his fatwā in a central concept of Islamic theology and practice. It was jihad that provides the grounds for the fatwā to kill all Americans—civilian and military—and their allies in any country in which it is possible to do so.

Historic Analogies

The closet analogy to bin Laden's position in the Christian tradition is the life and theology of the Crusaders. In the first Crusade (1096–99) during the Council of Clermont, Pope Urban II called upon all Christians to war against the Turks. He promised that those who died would receive remission of their sins. In this instance sincere

---

[21] Laqueur, *Voices of Terror*, 411.

believers whose piety was genuine, and whose actions were endorsed by legitimate ecclesiastical mandates, carried out the vicious killing of innocent civilians. These believers were not an isolated minority; and their claims and action was worked into a narrative of Christian history that was profoundly persuasive within the bounds of the church at the time. Other analogies can be found in the post-Reformation period among Protestants. Thomas Müntzer (1489–1525), one of the radical reformers, gladly massacred the inhabitants of Weinsberg in the name of God. Luther recommended in response that the German princes should wash their hands in the blood of the radical reformers and their followers. 100,000 peasants died in 1524 alone. In these instances believers did not simply use religion or the debris of religion for political and military purposes. The violence involved was rooted in, motivated by, and warranted by religious and theological convictions.

Remnants of this kind of attitude show up in Christian circles today. I recall vividly a dinner in Belfast when I was a student. A veteran missionary administrator was trying to recruit my wife and I to be missionaries among unevangelized tribes. We discussed the rioting that had broken out in the city. There was a pause before our guest noted with great solemnity: "You know those Catholics who live up the Falls Road. I am like David of old. I hate them with a perfect hatred." The comment sent chills down my spine at the time.

To be sure, all sorts of other factors and considerations play a role in brutality motivated by religious convictions. Thus the agents involved are happy to settle old scores, play upon issues of ethnic and national identity, and rape women. They come home loaded with loot, give vent to their savagery, and reorganize the map of the world. All this shows is that their actions were over-determined; they sprang from multiple reasons, motives, and causes. This is the norm in the deployment of violence; we should expect exactly the same in the case of Islamist terrorism.

This is precisely what we find there. In engaging in terrorism, Islamist fighters believe that they are liberating the oppressed, undermining the hegemony of the West, and cleansing the world of sensual filth. They are convinced that they are giving the United States of America a bloody nose. Bin Laden even thought that he was justified in engaging in acts of terrorism because this is appropriate retaliation for numerous acts of aggression against the *ummah*, the global Islamic community, over the last two centuries. Terrorism, as he saw it, is a matter of justice.

However, for bin Laden far more was at stake than justice. In substance he clearly thought that killing innocent civilians was both logically and religiously valid. Such killing was logically valid. "So, as they [North Americans] kill us, without a doubt we have to kill them, until we obtain a balance of terror."[22] It was religiously valid because "it has been laid down by the Prophet in an authentic tradition…"[23] To be sure, there are verses in the Qur'an that forbid killing children and innocents, but this is "not set in stone and there are other writings that uphold it."[24] Thus: "God's saying: 'And if you punish (your enemy, O you believers in the Oneness of God) then punish them with the like of that with which you were afflicted…'"[25] Moreover, there are recognized Muslim scholars and people of knowledge, like Ibn Taymiyyah, who share his interpretation of the relevant texts. The aim, of course, is in part deterrence. "We treat others like they treat us. Those who kill our women and our innocent, we kill their women and innocent, until they stop doing so." This is entirely natural. But it in no way undermined the religious sanction bin Laden deployed for killing innocent civilians. The religious sanction complements the motive of deterrence; the latter does not eradicate the former.

In the end bin Laden came clean and owned up to the commitment to terrorism.

> These young men that have sacrificed themselves in New York and Washington, these are the ones that speak the truth of the conscience of our *umma*, and they are its living conscience, which sees that it is imperative to take revenge against the evil doers and transgressors and criminals and terrorists, who terrorize the true believers. So, not all terrorism is restrained or ill-advised. There is terrorism that is ill-advised and there is terrorism that is a good act. So, in the definition of the word, if a criminal or a thief feels that he is terrorized by the police, do we label the police terrorists and say they terrorized the thief? No, the terrorism of the police towards the criminals is a good act, and the terrorism that is being exercised by the criminals against

[22] Bruce Lawrence, *Messages to the World: The Statements of Osama bin Laden* (New York: Verso, 2005), 114.
[23] Ibid.
[24] Ibid.
[25] Ibid.

the true believers is wrong and ill-advised. So America and Israel practice ill-advised terrorism, and *we practice good terrorism*, because it deters those from killing our children in Palestine and other places.[26]

It is clear where this evidence lands us. It confirms the conclusion that we reached earlier on the basis of the piety, exegetical beliefs, and theological convictions of the terrorists of 9/11. Osama bin Laden and the al-Qaeda operatives in New York were not Muslims who happened to be terrorists; they are Islamist terrorists. They were self-confessed terrorists motivated and warranted by a sincere vision of Islam; and they were self-confessed Muslims who insisted that their terrorism was morally, logically, and religiously valid. We are not dealing with nationalists or with radical activists who were using the faith and practice of Islam as a mechanism of rhetoric or self-deception; we are dealing with terrorists embedded in a form of Islam that is widespread, deep, informed, articulate, and fully conscious of its own piety and legitimacy.

This is a startling and uncomfortable truth. It is very tempting to evade the force of it by insisting that this cannot be the case because Islam is a religion of peace; so Osama bin Laden cannot be an authentic Muslim. We can understand why politicians reach for this language. They rightly want folk to stay calm in the midst of ignorance and prejudice. There is a time, however, when we must be candid and speak the truth. Aside from the fact that bin Laden rightly protested that he had not committed any of the well-known great sins of Islam "in full knowledge that this is one of the wrongful actions in religion,"[27] the move by politicians to speak of peace when there is no peace simply does not fit the evidence. There are various streams of Islam. Within those streams adherents of one highly potent current do not hesitate to engage in acts of terrorism and to seek warrant and inspiration in their religious faith for their actions.

The Majority Report

It would, however, be equally wrong to go to the opposite extreme and say that Islam is a religion of violence and that here we have the proof of it. This only holds if bin Laden and his colleagues were representative of Islam as a whole. We can now turn formally to that

[26] Ibid., 120, emphasis mine.
[27] Ibid., 121.

issue. Is this vision of Islam representative of Islam or is it a fringe version of Islam? Is it mainstream or is it unconventional? Is it the majority report or is it a minority report? The answer is equally clear: it is not representative of Islam as a whole; it is a minority report.

The evidence for this crucial judgment is decisive.

For one thing, Muslim leaders across the world have publicly and repeatedly repudiated the vision and action of Osama bin Laden and al-Qaeda.[28] In the wake of 9/11 hundreds of Muslim leaders, scholars, converts, and institutes made it abundantly clear that they totally rejected the killing of innocent civilians in New York and elsewhere. The terrible murders of 9/11 were dismissed as gross crimes, sinful acts, and shameless evils; they were totally rejected as cowardly, deserving condemnation, treasonous, suicidal, unjustifiable, and barbaric. President Muhammad Khatani of Iran wrote: "The September 11 terrorist blasts in America can only be the job of a group that have voluntarily severed their own ears and tongues, so that the only language with which they could communicate would be destroying and spreading death."[29] Yusuf Islam (formerly Cat Stevens, the pop star) in a press release stated: "While it is still not clear who carried out the attack, it must be stated that no right thinking follower of Islam could possibly condone such an action: the Qur'an equates the murder of one innocent person with the murder of the whole of humanity."[30] Those who kill innocent civilians are roundly condemned as having deviant beliefs and misleading ideologies; they are acting counter to the humanitarian values of Islam; they do not understand Islam, having no other faculty except ignorance and hatred; they do not reflect Muslim beliefs and practices; they are murderers, terrorists, extremists, radicals, and fundamentalists, who have inflicted a horrible scar on the history of Islam and humanity.

Second, bin Laden's defense of terrorism was repudiated by the classical teaching of Islam on the practice of war. Islam, of course,

---

[28] For a collection of relevant material see http://kurzman.unc.edu/islamic-statments-against-terrorism/ [accessed 01/06/2013]. See also 153 Saudi Intellectuals, "How We Can Co-exist," in David Blankenhorn, Abdou Filali-Ansary, Hassan I. Mneimneh, Alex Roberts, eds., *The Islam/West Debate* (New York: Rowan and Littlefield, 2005), 65–180.

[29] Address to the United Nations General Assembly, November 9, 2001.

[30] Press release of September 13, 2001.

considers war a duty under certain conditions; one is obliged to go to war to end oppression when all other measures fail. One can also go to war in order to promote the advancement of Muslim power. However the relevant factors for the current issue have to do not with the conditions for waging war but with the clear injunctions on the conduct of war. Thus the killing of innocents is not allowed, nor is the wanton destruction of livestock, animals, orchards, trees, and wells. This tradition of restraint runs all the way from Muhammad right up to the present. It is the central teaching of Islam across space and time, across its divisions past and present. Not even the famous sword text can be stretched to cover acts of terrorism. "Then when the Sacred Months are over, kill the idolaters wherever you find them, take them as captives, besiege them, and lie in wait for them at every point of observation. If they repent afterwards, perform the prayer and pay the alms, then release them…"(9:5) The harshest text in Islam clearly confines the injunction to kill to idolaters; it does not extend to the killing of innocent civilians.

The judgment that bin Laden and his cohorts are not mainstream Muslims is confirmed by the language that has now become commonplace. Thus he is systematically described as a radical, and his vision of Islam is now conventionally referred to as 'Islamism' rather than simply 'Islam'. His theology and practice represented a minority report within Islam as a whole. It belongs within the wider diversity that has long been the case within the history of Islam. It stands at the polar opposite of the vision of liberal Islam that is now being vigorously pursued as a live option within the West. Radical Islam is a live option, but it is a live option alongside several other versions of Islam.

It is very difficult for mainstream Muslims to get out the message that radical Islam is a minority report within Islam as a whole. Indeed they face something of a public relations nightmare. The media generally are much more interested in radical Islam. The part is often confused with the whole; there are a lot of critics of Islam who are happy to present it in the worst possible light; and it is not always good form to attack fellow Muslims in public. The truth of the matter, however, is patently clear: radical Islam is not mainstream Islam.

It is certainly good news that the faith and practice of Osama bin Laden is a minority report within Islam. Islam is a religion with over a billion believers; if Osama bin Laden and al-Qaeda represented its mainstream teaching and practice, we would be in boiling water.

The Fanaticism of Terrorist Minorities

However, we are not yet on dry land. Terrorist groups will always be a minority within a bigger majority. We know from the Irish situation that a minority can still wreck horrendous havoc. We also know how devilishly difficult it has been to eradicate and contain terrorism even in Ireland. In the Irish case we were dealing with a small group of about 500 terrorists, whose primary goals were political and finite, and whose current leaders were prepared to enter into negotiation and compromise.[31] Their fanaticism was deep and protracted; but it had a bottom line. The fanaticism of Islamist terrorists has no bottom line because it is grounded in faith and divine revelation. Hence it has no difficulty, for example, in reworking suicide bombers into martyrs who gladly take on the task of killing innocent civilians. The closest we came to this in Ireland was the case of the murder bomb. In this instance the terrorists would kidnap a family, strap the male head of the family into a van full of explosives, threaten to kill the rest of his family if he did not drive the van to the chosen target, and then detonate the bomb when he arrived at it, killing the driver in the process. The terrorists themselves went home to eat their supper and play with the dog; there was no question of their committing suicide. In the case of radical Islam this is taken one step further. Here terrorists are fully prepared to kill themselves to kill others; they can legitimately profess the first order language of religion, that of martyrdom, as they do so.

The scale and the intensity of terrorism within Islam fit with the theological grounding invoked. The idea at work here is very simple; it is missed again and again by those who have lost the ability to read theological texts and cannot see the rationality that is operating within radical Islam.[32] If it is God who lies behind the mandate to kill, then the faithful believer must kill; there is a duty to kill. What is at stake is the infallible will of God rather than the mandate

---

[31]Not that all is plain sailing; terrorist groups continue to exist. In a period of seven months in 2006 dissident bomb attacks cost close to a staggering $50 million dollars in Northern Ireland.

[32]Most recently in Lee Harris, *The Suicide of Reason: Radical Islam's Threat to the West* (New York: Basic Books, 2007).

of fallible, human agents. The strength of the divine mandate far outstrips that of a human mandate. This is a purely general point of logic that stands secure, for God does not make mistakes and obedience to his commands is obligatory. Now add in the promises attached to this, say, that killing will bring about immediate forgiveness of sins, instantaneous entry into paradise, and the welcome of beautiful women standing ready to satisfy. In these circumstances the response will not just be morally obligatory but also spiritually and humanly attractive.

There are so many other factors at work that we can readily miss this crucial religious dimension. Radical Islamists detest Western materialism, imperialism, and colonialism, and they want to preserve their own traditional culture. They hate all things Jewish. They rail against the effects of globalization in its many forms. They have a profound sense of grievance from past wrongs, military defeats, and humiliations. They have memories of crusades from long ago. They entertain fantasies of military victory inspired by the defeat of the Russians in Afghanistan. They see North America as the great Satan and are keenly aware of the use and abuse of American military power. They are apt to buy into conspiracy theories. All these factors provide an explosive cocktail of causes and reasons to strike out in violence and retaliation. They are not, however, the whole story; we are myopic if we restrict ourselves to them. We must also attend to the theological foundations of Islam. When the aforementioned considerations are combined with the intensities of piety and faith, then we face an extraordinary challenge.

The Liberal Reformists

The challenge would certainly be manageable if radical Islam was confined to the traditional homelands of Islam. That horse is no longer confined to the stable. Globalization, immigration, and public declarations of war have brought the challenge right inside the West. Nobody knows how to quantify what is at stake. Pundits proliferate; shrill autobiographical warnings abound; think-tanks are hard at work. Sentimentalists look the other way and set their hope on more politics; realists prepare for the worst-case scenario and cross their fingers. I know one expert on Islam who is glad that most Muslims are nominal and not very serious about their faith. There are enough signs of danger to make the most optimistic wary. In October 2006, MI5 (the British secret service) in England was keeping 1,600 individuals under surveillance. Dame Eliza Manninger-Buller, who was once head of MI5, uncharacteristically warned in public that threats included the use of chemical, bacteriological agents, radioactive materials, and even nuclear technology. This is one reason why the Obama administration is worried about the future of biological weapons in the civil war in Syria. Dame Eliza identified no less than 200 groups who were actively engaged in plotting, or facilitating terrorists attacks in England or overseas.[33] Her agents were aware of 30 plots to kill people or damage the economy.[34] A larger catalogue of woe can be compiled for the United States.[35]

There is another woe beneath this woe. Folk really worry that even at its best Islam poses a threat in that Islam is a robust missionary religion with a stout political ideology. Both elements scare us.

On the one hand, Islam is sufficiently sure of itself to want to convert everybody to its faith. We are not dealing here with devout, muddled Anglicans, the cuddly Labradors of the Christian religion, who live and let live. It is much more like we are dealing with aggressive fundamentalist Baptists, the pit bulls of evangelical religion, who are out to convert the world. Even then, this analogy is unfair. The Muslims I meet in Dallas and elsewhere are not just witty, courteous, and professionally competent; they are also brimming with self-confidence in the truth of their faith. Most Christians by comparison are intellectually sloppy and uninformed; they barely know the first principles and practices of their religion.

On the other hand, we have hoary memories of Islam as a missionary religion that readily moved with the power of the sword eastward and westward in order to clear a space for the hearing of the Word of God through the Qur'an. There was indeed no compulsion in religion, but this did nothing to stay the mandate to conquer the world. The no compulsion rule was restricted to the matter of personal faith; no one was forced to convert. The conquering was a social and political reality, and it was within that reality that the option to convert or not to convert was exercised. It was within the social and political world of Islam that there was no personal com-

[33] This is a conservative estimate; the number is now almost certainly higher.
[34] BBC News website accessed on 10 October, 2006.
[35] See Bruce Hoffman, *Inside Terrorism* (New York: Columbia University Press, 2006), and Steven Emerson, *Jihad Incorporated: A Guide to Militant Islam in the US* (New York: Prometheus Books, 2006).

pulsion. Even then the alternatives were stark. One could convert to Islam; if one was a Jew or a Christian, one could suffer the fate of second-class citizenship and accept *dhimmi* status; or one could be killed. The ultimate aim was to extend the dār al Islam (realm of Islam) until the dār al Harb (realm of war; those territories not under Islamic rule) was conquered and brought within the fold of Islam. Behind the hoary memories lies the Word of the Qur'an, a revelation that cannot be overturned under any circumstances. Suddenly we are not just worried about terrorist attacks; we are grasping for the air we breathe.

The challenge of clearing the air and opening the windows of Islam has, of course, been taken up by those who seek to liberalize Islam in a way similar to what has happened in Christianity. They rightly insist that religious traditions are not static monuments but living, dynamic organisms that can adjust to new situations and circumstances. So they hope that Islam can shed its more militant teachings and practices and become the moderate, peace-loving, justice-seeking religion that it was always meant to be.[36] This movement within Islam is extraordinarily important. There is far more to it than the move from a literal to a figurative or symbolic interpretation of the Qur'an. The strategy involves a fundamental reworking of the basic doctrines of Islam.

Compared to Liberal forms of Christianity, where there is a tendency to give away the store, the internal reformation of Islam is much more modest, but it is still substantial. I recently met a brilliant young lawyer from Algeria who was visiting Dallas on an internship that was part of a six-month immersion program. She took no prisoners in her defense of Islam but was equally adamant in her vision of what it involved. For one thing, she insisted on coming to terms with our shared human values as represented by just war. She had difficulty fathoming the commitment to pacifism on the part of some Christians, but it was clear that in time she could work out why this was a live option in the Christian tradition. She took seriously the conscience of those who differed with her on important moral issues. She was resolute in her opposition to radical Islam in

---

[36] See Tariq Ramadan, *Western Muslims and the Future of Islam* (Oxford: Oxford University Press, 2004), Charles Kurzman, ed., *Liberal Islam, a Source Book* (New York: Oxford University Press, 1998); Reza Aslan, *No God but God* (New York: Random House, 2005); Khaled Abou El Fadl, *Islam and the Challenge of Democracy* (Princeton: Princeton University Press, 2004).

Algeria where well over 100,000 people had been killed. Following the French model on the relation between religion and politics, she had no time for religion-based political parties. She rejected polygamy as a serious option, arguing the case from the Qur'an on the grounds that genuine equality between the wives in a polygamous arrangement was not possible in today's world. She was totally open to modern culture in relation to technology, business, national customs, dress, and the like. She argued with gusto that individuals had to be free to develop their own interpretation of the Qur'an and the hadith. She had no time for gender inequality. Yet her identity as a Muslim was robust and secure. She was clear that Islam had a core set of beliefs and practices that were not negotiable. She was not for sale at any price when it came to the fundamentals of Islam and to her identity as a Muslim.

We can expect to hear more from Liberals within Islam over the next generation. The odds in favor of it may, however, be long ones, so we should move forward with caution. The analogy with developments within modern Christianity is worth pondering. Think of it along these lines. Optimistic Protestants have set out again and again to fix the faith once and for all, but the results have been a very mixed bag. Martin Luther had his hands full dealing with militants who were all too ready to massacre the enemy in the name of God. His own disposition towards Jews and those who disagreed with him was appalling. John Calvin was vicious in his attitude to those who disagreed with him; he did not hesitate to lend a hand in the execution of Servetus because he denied the doctrine of the Trinity. In the nineteenth century many Liberal Protestants took a very different tack and gave away the store in the drive to accommodate and adjust. They gave up on special divine revelation, miracles, and central Christian doctrines like the incarnation. Currently Liberal Protestantism is on the ropes, dying the death of a thousand qualifications. Liberationist forms of Christianity have displaced it; these in turn are being sidelined by the worldwide resurgence of Evangelicalism and the invention of Pentecostalism. In the meantime Roman Catholicism has lived on, recovered its conservative confidence, and found fresh ways to stake out its ancient claims. Eastern Orthodoxy steadily stays the course without any signs of reform. Looking back across this history, it is much too early in the game to predict that Liberal versions of Islam will survive across the generations. They may well fail. Like their first cousins within Liberal Protestantism they may do more to pave the way for a shift into secular faiths than to preserve Islam. Even so it is of the utmost importance in the short term that Liberal forms of Islam be developed and flourish.

Efforts at radical reinterpretation of the original texts and sources in religion cut both ways. Indeed Osama bin Laden inhabited a tradition of Islam that in its own way has taken the measure of Liberal agendas. That tradition is well aware of Enlightenment proposals and the double-edged sword they entail for religion. Thus the Enlightenment can kill off religion by privatization, by offers of freedom, and by taking control of public education, as has happened in much of the West. The strategy is first to tame and tolerate, then to domesticate and deter, and finally to suffocate and strangle by means of legal enactment. Protestant theologians have been all too ready to offer themselves as the agents of such change in their churches. They play the part of sacrificial lambs in wolves' clothing. Alternatively, the Enlightenment can destroy religion by the simple method of killing religious believers, as happened in Russia and elsewhere. Bin Laden and his radical colleagues took the measure of modern communism, nationalism, and soft secular totalitarianism. They have been only too ready to provide a comprehensive political alternative to secular political ideologies, including the option of representative democracy. Modern western democracy and capitalism are not a problem for radical Islam, as we can see in the case of Algeria and in the Palestinian Territories, where radical Islamists have been successful in winning elections. In the former case they were prevented from taking office by the army who created space for a more moderate version of Islam. In the latter case they are another bridge to the Islamisization of the area. It is naïve to think that it will be plain sailing for Liberal Islam. Radical Islam in its own way is in fact a form of reformation. Its proponents are hell bent on the restoration of the earliest version of Islam and they clearly have a fair amount of wind behind their backs at this point in history.

Radical Islamists have also taken the measure of the spiritual alienation that haunts so much of the Muslim world and of the West. Reading the sermons of Abu Ala Maududi and the popular writings of Sayed Qutb is like reading the sermons and publications of many revivalists and preachers within Christianity. They speak from the heart; they understand the spiritual anxieties of their hearers; and they articulate the emptiness of modern atheism and secularism. They write with dignity and flair; they speak a word of hope in a world of cruelty and despair; they are brimful of piety and faith; they have anchors that go deep into the human soul; and they are more than ready to die for the faith once delivered to the faithful. Modern reformers may well be left behind in this revival and resurgence of lively faith. This is certainly what is happening in Christianity outside Europe. The current mood and trend favors the revivalists and radicals as much as it does the Liberal revisionists.[37]

It would be foolish to bet the store simply on the Liberal reworking of Islam as the way of the future. I respect those who hope that this may be the case; we can expect that their tribe will grow and flourish; but so too will the good fortunes of conservative and radical versions of Islam.

Radical Muslims used airplanes as flying bombs to blow up buildings and kill the innocent. The spiritual preparations they carried out on the eve of 9/11 and the theology they embody run the risk of exploding the conventional foundations of politics and civil society. We know where radical Islamists stand on the relation between religion and politics. We are on our way to finding out where Liberal-minded Muslims are headed. We have yet to tackle the stance of mainstream, traditional Islam.

We are now leaving the wasteland of Manhattan and wandering into the grandiose corridors of power in the White House, in Washington D.C., and in the political capitals of Europe.

---

[37] For a fascinating account of pacific Islam see Lamin O. Sanneh, *Summoned from the Margin: Homecoming of an African* (Grand Rapids, Mich: William B. Eerdmans Pub. Co, 2012), 191-208..

4

Life is Short, Nasty, and Irish

Theologians in Action

Changing a famous aphorism of Thomas Hobbes, a witty Dublin student once remarked that life is short, nasty, and British.

In September 2006 I visited Nepal, a country whose people, given their affection for Britain, would hesitate to accept the alteration to the saying. On the first evening in Katmandu I took off on my own to explore the area close to my hotel. I managed to make it past the first battery of drug dealers and rickshaw cyclists, and headed down a street to the right. Immediately I was stopped by a young gentleman trader in the doorway of a store replete with shirts, pashminas, carpets, chess sets, and other tourist items. He had instantly taken a shine to my bushy beard. Initially I dismissed this interest as a sales ploy, but decided to go along. Within minutes we had struck up a friendship.

Farouk is a devout Muslim. His family is from Kashmir; his father had opened the store a generation before him; he knows seven languages and speaks English with ease; he was full of curiosity about Ireland and America; he introduced me to his friends. On every free evening while I was in Katmandu, we met for tea in his store. If it was time for his prayers, we paused until he was finished, and then went back to our conversation. We freely talked from the heart about anything that came into our heads, including our faith. On the final evening when I visited him, there was a torrential downpour. I had forgotten my umbrella; he enthusiastically loaned me his; and he was soaked to the skin in escorting me back to my hotel by a shorter route.

In the course of my visits Farouk tried to convert me to Islam. This was done naturally and in a pleasing manner. Knowing my work as a professor, he decided to bring me some publications from the local mosque to peruse. He brought me material on the nature of the Qur'an, on the historical mistakes in the bible, and on the compatibility between science and Islam. Much of this was popular and superficial. What really caught my eye was a volume by the Egyptian theologian Sayed Qutb, whom I had been reading on and off for months. The volume was entitled *Social Justice in Islam*. I had not read it and was keen to buy it, so that I could read it on the plane journey home; regrettably the copy was from the mosque library and was only available on loan. I do not know if Farouk has studied Qutb seriously; he certainly has the intelligence to do so. For me it added a mysterious layer to our friendship.

Sayed Qutb's book caught my eye because he was one of the leading architects of recent radical Islamist theology. His brother was one of the teachers of Osama bin Laden. I was surprised to find his work so readily available in English in Katmandu. This is a very long way from Egypt, Qutb's home base. I was even more surprised when I discovered on my return to Dallas that Qutb's work was on the curriculum for high schoolers in the mosque close to my home. When I expressed skepticism to the journalist who told me this, he readily removed it by producing the relevant public records.

Clearly the arrival of militant and robust forms of Islam in the West poses a whole new challenge to the social and political status quo. The good news is that we have had centuries of experience working through the relationship between full-bodied forms of religion and politics. Yet we cannot assume in advance that the conventional means of resolving the foundational disputes that arise will continue to work in the case of Islam. They may well do so, but we cannot assume they will. The conventional wisdom as we have worked it out in the West is simple: we need a filtering system to keep out toxic material.

Over the years the West has developed a variety of filtering systems designed to keep the public square from being flooded with explosive ideas and practices, especially those derived from religion. The initial impetus for this came in the aftermath of the wars of religion set in motion by the Reformation. The troubles in Ireland reflect the deposit of earlier disputes in which it was assumed that politics served the cause of true religion and religion underwrote the cause of what was politically correct. England got really serious about Ireland in the late sixteenth century when it became clear that Ireland could be used as a stepping-stone for Spain to get to England, undo the English Reformation, and return Catholic power to its rightful place on the throne. Religious and geopolitical interests can be logically distinguished but they were materially inseparable. In fact the move into Ireland in the plantation of Ulster during 1610–1640 was at one and the same time a colonial act, an effort to eradicate popery, a defensive invasion, a missionary exercise, and an extension of the long-standing conflict with Rome. The various massacres that resulted from this conflict at places like Portadown and Drogheda are still part of the painful memories of people in Ireland.

It is worth stepping back into the time of Elizabeth I to see afresh the ferocity evoked by the threat to political stability from religious commitment. In February 1570 Pope Pius V made an official ruling in *Regnans in Excelsus* in which Elizabeth (the "pretended Queen of England") was excommunicated. He thereby released English Catholics from their allegiance to her and openly encouraged her overthrow. In these circumstances the Jesuit mission to take back England for Roman Catholicism was an extraordinary one that required great dexterity and discipline. Elizabeth and her ministers were more than a match for it. The ruthlessness deployed was dramatic and abundant; it was directed both against priests and ordinary lay people.[38] Here are two examples that make the point graphically.

Edmund Campion (1540–1581) had a brilliant career at Oxford as an Anglican before converting to Rome and becoming a dedicated Jesuit. Sent back to England disguised as a jewel dealer to reclaim Protestants to the true faith, he was arrested on 17 July 1581. Queen Elizabeth, who had earlier been dazzled by his brilliance on a visit to Oxford, personally interviewed him in hopes of changing his mind. He was offered all sorts of inducements to recant, tortured on the rack, and forced to debate for four hours without chair,

---

[38] For a riveting narration of this see Alice Hogge, *God's Secret Agents* (New York: HarperCollins, 2005).

table, or notes. His old skills as a scholar had not deserted him; he confounded his opponents. He was then tried for treason, more precisely for conspiracy to murder Queen Elizabeth; the verdict was a foregone conclusion. On 1 December he was led to Tyburn in driving rain and there hung, drawn, and quartered before the assembled crowd. At his trial he had been so badly tortured that he could not raise his right arm to take the oath; by the time of his execution all his nails had already been plucked from his fingers.

Around 1574 Margaret Clitherow converted to Catholicism at the age of 18. Already married, she used her home as a refuge for itinerating priests. On March 10, 1586 she was arrested for harboring priests. She refused to plead guilty or not guilty. Following ancient legal precedent, her refusal was read as a guilty plea, and she was solemnly sentenced. She was to be taken to the lowest part of the prison, stripped naked, laid down with her back upon the ground, and as much weight laid upon her as she was able to bear. This was to be kept up for three days without meat or drink, except for a little barley and puddle water. Then on the third day, her hands and feet were to be tied to a post, a sharp stone was to be placed under her back, and she was to be pressed to death. On March 25 the officials expedited the ordeal. They put a sharp stone the size of a fist beneath her naked body, put a wooden panel on top of her, and placed a weight of close to nine hundred pounds on top of the panel. Her ribs were broken; they burst through her skin; mercifully she was dead within fifteen minutes.

Reworking the Foundations

It was only a matter of time before somebody called all this brutality and bloodletting into question. The questioning came from within the bosom of Christianity itself. Luther, Calvin, and Erasmus' superiors in Rome may have drowned out any courageous plea for tolerance and moderation, but over time the call to tolerance got off the ground.[39] The story is a complex one, but it is vital to note one neglected feature of the revolution in thought that became second nature in disputes about the relation between faith and politics in the West. The Reformation debates were not just debates about this or that theological proposal; they were also debates about how to resolve theological proposals. Protestants staked all on scripture in

[39] For a fine account of Erasmus on tolerance see Stefan Zweig, *Erasmus of Rotterdam* (New York: Garden City, 1937).

various ways; Roman Catholics went beyond scripture to appeal to the authority of the church. In both cases everything hung on the authority of divine revelation; each side had hit rock bottom and could not budge.

René Descartes (1596–1650) and John Locke (1632–1704) saw that a neat way to bypass this impasse was to go for a very different criterion, namely the appeal to reason. For Descartes this meant first and foremost an appeal to rational intuition; for Locke it meant an appeal to experience. This looks very secular, of course, but it is a soft rather than hard version of secularism, for the secular was offered up as a servant and foundation of the theological. The assumption was ingenious: once we really know how to adjudicate between truth and falsehood, then we can go back to the business of resolving our moral and theological disputes in a rational manner. Descartes offered his work as a contribution to the Theology Faculty in the University of Paris; Locke was driven in his deliberations by the chaos he had witnessed first-hand of the religious believers in England. Both of them were trying to solve a problem that was through and through theological. They were pious believers who were fed up with fighting; they invented a whole new philosophical tradition to break loose from the impasse that was causing death and destruction.

The lure of these alternatives was irresistible. First, the turn to reason and experience cut off any dogmatic appeal to divine revelation. Now the identification of true revelation and its interpretation had to be resolved by appeal to reason; otherwise those proposing divine revelation were engaging in intellectual hand waving and in the reading of arbitrary texts. So reason became foundational and paved the way for the exercise of rationality. Second, introducing reason and experience introduced a note of peace and quiet into the discussion. It is hard to reason if you are all hot and bothered; even more so if you want to settle disputes using a gun. So the model of the rational person using a proper rational methodology that transcends the partisan commitments of religious believers began to take root as a way of living life, and more importantly, as a way of doing politics. Third, the turn to reason underwrote a pleasing self-confidence in those who believe in it. It is flattering to think of ourselves as rational animals, as intelligent agents, as autonomous thinkers, and as free to make up our own minds about contested issues.

We know this revolution in thinking as the Enlightenment. At a political level the Enlightenment was implemented in a wide variety of ways. In England and Scotland the leading Christian churches remained established, but other groups were tolerated so long as they did not disrupt the basic political orders of the day. Initially there was a confessional state in which it was a requirement of office that one held to the doctrine of the Trinity. In addition, Oxford and Cambridge universities were confessional universities open only to Trinitarian Christian teachers and students. Over time the conditions of participation were changed so that anyone could teach in the universities, stand for public office, and serve in the government.

In the United States there was a different arrangement summed up in the felicitous language of the initial clause of the First Amendment of the Constitution of the United States of America. "Congress shall make no law respecting an establishment of religion, or prohibiting the free exercise thereof…" The case for this proposal has been argued both in terms of the vices of establishing any religion and in terms of the virtues of permitting the free exercise of religion. We may haggle about the exact meaning, and we may debate forever about how to apply this formula. However, there is no question but that this is generally seen as the gold standard for any serious account of the relation between religion and the state.

Separating Church and State

It took the Christian churches a long time to accept this critical distinction between religion and the state along with the complex network of practices that operate as a filtering system in the relation between the two. They could do so in the end with a good conscience because they had the internal resources within the Christian tradition to do so. To begin with, the Christian faith started as a movement within Judaism that was persecuted for three centuries by the Roman state. It did not need the state to be itself; indeed it thrived and spread in part because of persecution. In this Christianity was like Judaism before it, for Israel's foundational document, the Torah, makes it clear that Israel existed before the settlement in the Promised Land. Second, Christians generally had a very robust vision of divine providence with which they could look upon the actions of the state as an agent of God in supplying order and justice. Paul famously insisted that even the powers of Pagan Rome were ordained of God and should be obeyed. Third, Christians looked to the life beyond as the fulfillment of its deepest hopes for human existence, so they could keep their distance from the life and work of the state without strain. They could live with the mistakes and madness of political life. Fourth, both the corruption that came with the establishment of religion and the bloody wars that erupted with the destabilizing of Christianity brought about by the Reformation drove many Christians to welcome the separation of church and state. The separation kept religious believers from imposing their views on non-believers; and it kept believers and their churches free of government interference.

There were other considerations that lent weight to these factors. The practices of holding councils, assemblies, and conferences, of electing leaders, of developing canon law, of building and sustaining universities, all these created dispositions and skills that were valuable in government and politics. Christian theologians readily worked out fresh ways to underwrite the separation of church and state, so doubts about the agreed arrangements could be met and new, unforeseen problems could be addressed. The appeal to reason, the privileging of settling disputes without recourse to violence, fitted with the Christian ethic of love to the neighbor. A vision of human agents as made in the image of God now represented by the use of reason made it a good thing to apply one's mind to political problems. A guarded sense that freedom was somehow essential to proper human fulfillment played well in a political world that was built on freedom. The Protestant recovery of lay vocation made politics an honorable profession in its own right. The strong sense of pessimism latent in Christian doctrines of sin welcomed checks and balances that curbed human pride and the abuse of power. The hope engendered by the Christian belief in redemption spilled over into a readiness to engage in the political arena despite its nastiness and corruption. Success in implementing religiously inspired values, ideas, and policies in law, education, and in the ethos of society encouraged a commitment to democratic institutions across the generations. Even failure helped; it created the motivation for further political action and activism to fix society.

Pressures Within and Without

The filtering system designed to manage the flow of religion into the public water has worked exceptionally well. The institutions and practices that are in place are an astonishing human achievement that is vital in representative democracies where folk disagree deeply on the nature and ends of human existence. From the beginning, however, the filtering system was subject to intense pressure. The materials flowing through the mechanism can easily surge to breaking point; and the mechanism itself can be damaged relatively easily.

Take the materials flowing from the side of religion. The Christian religion has a strong political impulse at its very core. It insists that there is but one Lord who stands over all earthly lords. On the one hand, the subversive sense of a divine mandate naturally poses a challenge to all governments; which is one reason why politicians readily try to tame it, destroy it, or co-opt it. On the other hand, it is easy for Christians to identify their political convictions with the will of God and knowingly or unknowingly seek to implement them in the political arena. Furthermore, religion calls forth a hearty response, engaging the heart as well as the head. It can be emotionally difficult to hold back from using secular power to further noble causes. Self-righteousness can readily override humility; holy triumphalism can easily be revved up to occupy enemy territory. All of this is aided and abetted by the sense that Christianity is true and underwritten by divine revelation. Thus to challenge faith can quickly be taken as a challenge not to the fallible human agent who speaks for faith but to the very Word of God. Those who disagree are seen as enemies of truth and a threat to the very Word of God; they can be demonized and sent off to hell where they belong.

Consider now the crucial mechanism at the core of the filtering system that is supposed to keep these forces in check, that is, human reason disconnected from tradition, and reduced to entirely secular methods that allow no appeal to divine revelation. This is the crucial safety net in the system as a whole. On the one hand, if reason in this sense is taken at face value, it is very narrow in scope, excluding materials that are vital to making political decisions. Thus political reason makes use of moral discernment and visions of human nature that are very much the preserve of theology. The hot button issues of marriage, abortion, the death penalty, welfare benefits, prison conditions, educational policy, and the like, cannot be addressed, much less resolved, without widening the gauge of the net and allowing through material on which political decisions have always depended. The professed secularism has been little more than skin deep more often than not. We can see this in the general ethos of the United States over the years. The United States is certainly not a Christian nation, if we mean by that, that it has an established church, or that it operates consciously on the basis of Christian values. Yet, the footprints of the Christian faith show up all over the place, that is, in its calendar, its public holidays, its charitable tax policies, its vision of marriage, its public iconography, the history of its private colleges and universities, and in its political speech and discourse. It is certainly more Protestant than it is Catholic, and it certainly more Christian than it is Hindu, Buddhist, or Islamic. The safety net has been constricted and widened at will depending on the actual elected officials and civil servants in play.

On the other hand, the notion of reason as something purely procedural and neutral is extremely fragile. There was a dark side to the Enlightenment that is now becoming visible. At the outset David Hume (1711–1776) rubbished reason by restricting it narrowly to mere deduction, and thus elbowed out not just belief in God but also belief in the ordinary world, in causation, and even in the self. In the nineteenth century the holy trinity of Frederick Nietzsche, Karl Marx, and Sigmund Freud, called into question the purity of reason in a host of ways. Appeals to reason were revealed as systems of passion, power, and repression that were better seen as acts of concealment than of illumination. In the twentieth century Hume was rediscovered and made the high priest of a purist appeal to natural science in Anglo-American Positivism, while Continental Philosophy created an alternative labyrinth of intellectual negativity if not nihilism in and around Paris. In the meantime consumerism and sensuality, always waiting in the wings, have flourished. Communism and fascism became substitute religions for many, readily filling the space vacated by Christian leaders who lost their intellectual nerve when the full force of reason was directed against the faith. Communists wrapped themselves triumphantly in the flag of economic reason; fascists wedded themselves to virulent forms of nationalism and racism; both deployed the resources of science and technology down to the last atom.

The old dream of destroying religion once and for all dies hard, of course, but the dream has become for many a nightmare. It is no surprise that robust religion is making a comeback. Liberalized versions of Christianity have little substantive to say spiritually and theologically, they can no longer camouflage their minimalism with confidence; they are often the invention of lapsed Fundamentalists who are still as strident and reactionary as their former selves.[40] A host of secular philosophies have been tried and found wanting; some of them have been (and still are) the engines of vast killing machines. Virulent forms of evangelical Christianity are flourishing; conservative versions of mainline Christianity are back in business. Adherents of these new movements within Christianity are no longer prepared to sit at home and baby-sit granny; they have walked into the public square equipped with an education and are ready to organize and speak up. Not surprisingly some secularists are becoming paranoiac, reaching in the name of their private philosophy paraded as science to write off religion as a contaminating disease.[41] Others are becoming more strident, reiterating the dogmas of the Enlightenment as the foundation of all human dignity and law.[42] Their way of dealing with Muslims mimics what they did with Christians: banish them to their own little private world and house-train them or castrate them on the way to the public forum.[43]

A Dogmatic, Ignorant Secularist

I was forcefully reminded of how nasty secularists can be on the same trip to Nepal where I became friends with Farouk. I had gone to Chitwan National Park with another Nepalese friend, and we were staying at a guesthouse that was also being used by a mature student from Copenhagen called Martin. We decided to have dinner together. After initial chitchat we began to share where we were from and what we did professionally. The mature student worked for a computer company while he studied part-time for a master's degree in physics. When he discovered that I taught theology he

[40] Bishop John Shelby Spong of the Episcopal Church, USA, is an obvious example.

[41] Most notably in Richard Dawkins, *The God Delusion* (Oxford: Oxford University Press, 2006).

[42] See Ronald Dworkin, *Is Democracy Possible Here?* (Princeton: Princeton University Press, 2006).

[43] For a very different treatment of the problem see Jeffrey Stout, *Democracy and Tradition* (Princeton: Princeton University Press, 2004) and Christopher J. Eberle, *Religious Conviction in Liberal Politics* (Cambridge: Cambridge University Press, 2002).

lost little time in getting down to business. He mentioned that he had long ago given up belief in magic. He most certainly had no time for fairy tales. He went on to insist that people who believed in God were clearly stupid; they had sent their brains on a permanent holiday and were not committed to evidence or reason. He continued in this vein until he ran out of negative things to say about religious belief.

At a suitable moment I began a series of questions. Had he read any of the Christian gospels? "No," he replied, "but I have recently seen a television program on the Gospel of Judas." I asked him if he had actually read the Gospel of Judas, noting that it was extremely short and could be easily found on the internet. He had not read it; and he did not need to do so. I suggested that he might find it interesting to read one of the gospels for himself. He adamantly insisted that this too would not be necessary. I proposed that before writing off the history of theology he might think of reading some of the giants of the tradition. Of course, he could not name a single serious theologian when pressed. He had no clue about the complexity and depth of theological debates. At that point I simply reported that I found him ignorant, illiterate, intellectually lazy, uninformed, and irrational. However, if he ever did decide to look into the subject seriously, say, by actually reading one of the gospels, he should ring me and reverse the charges. The rest of the evening went fine once we had cleared the air. My friend and I found a way through his defenses, but it was hard work given the genuine illiteracy and prejudice we encountered. No doubt Muslim believers would have found it every bit as difficult to get beyond the stereotypes of reason against fanaticism, of science against magic, and the standard farrago of nonsense that ignorant secularists too often display.

In the encounter with Islam in the West it is not going to be that easy this time around to keep religion out of politics by taking refuge in secularist ignorance and code words. The safety net is already showing signs of wear and tear; it may well be stretched to breaking point in the future.

Brutality Makes a Comeback

It is time to awaken from our political and secular slumbers. Earlier I noted two examples of brutality from the sixteenth century that alerted us to the depth of the problem. Consider now two more drawn from the recent past.

On September 27, 1996, young Taliban fighters, after entering Kabul, quickly found Hajibullah, the former president of Afghanistan. "He and his brother were beaten and tortured, castrated, dragged behind a jeep, shot, then hanged from a traffic pole in downtown Kabul. Cigarettes were placed in their mouths and money was stuffed in their pockets."[44] Sometime later the Taliban moved to retake Mazar-e-Sharif, home to a Shiite minority community, the Hazaras. They quickly killed the 1,500 soldiers guarding the city.

> Once inside the defenseless city, the Taliban continued raping and killing for two days, indiscriminately shooting anything that moved, then slitting the throats and shooting dead men in the testicles. The bodies of the dead were left to wild dogs for six days before survivors were allowed to bury them. Those citizens who fled the city on foot were bombed by the Taliban air force. Hundreds of others were loaded into shipping containers and baked alive in the desert sun.... Four hundred women were taken to be concubines.[45]

We are well beyond the brutality of Elizabethan England where Anglicans were happy to hang, draw and quarter Edmund Campion and crush Margaret Clitherow to death with a sharp stone busting through her ribs. The challenge to establishing even the semblance of democratic rule in Afghanistan is an enduring one. Like their allies in al-Qaeda, the Taliban are not interested in democracy. Al-Qaeda has made it very clear where it stands.

> The confrontation that we are calling for with the apostate regimes does not know Socratic debates...Platonic ideals....nor Aristotelian diplomacy. But it knows the dialogue of bullets, the ideals of assassination, bombing and destruction, and the diplomacy of the cannon and the machine gun. Islamic governments have never and will never be established through peaceful solutions and cooperative councils. They are established as they always have been by pen and gun, by word and bullet, by tongue and teeth.[46]

The Taliban were naturally overthrown by lethal force; in their case there were no resources within their version of Islam for mak-

---

[44]Lawrence Wright, *The Looming Tower: Al-Qaeda and the Road to 9/11* (New York: Alfred A. Knopf, 2006), 230.

[45]Ibid., 268.

[46]This is the opening section of their training manual, see Jerold M. Post, *Military Studies in the Jihad Against the Tyrants: The Al-Qaeda Training Manual* (Gardners Books, 2010).

ing the transition to tolerance. They threw away the filtering system for keeping religious toxic material out of the political water supply and took to fixing the problem with guns. Can the standard filtering system work in the case of mainstream versions of Islam?

Interrogating Mainstream Islam

We can ask this question in other ways. Can mainstream Muslims be assimilated into the political culture of the West? Are there the resources within Islam for making the transition to democracy that was made over time by Christianity? Will the standard policy of inclusivism work in the case of Islam?

The policy of inclusion has worked in the case of other religions and cultural traditions. Even the descendants of former slaves have been brought into the complex network of values and practices that are now essential to living together in a complicated, diverse world. They have accepted the distinction between church and state. They agree that there should be no established church and that there should be the free exercise of religion. They have bought into a social and civic world where there is free debate, tolerance, the rule of secular law, rituals of honor, offensive public behavior, great occasions of state, common flags and emblems, common schooling, privacy, pavement politics, and religious elbow room. They have accepted more or less the conventional filtering system for keeping toxic religious material out of the political whirlpool. Will the system work in the case of Islam?

The crux of the issue is simple: mainstream Islam is a robust religion with a clear political ideology that rejects the separation of religion and politics, of church and state, and thus by its very nature overwhelms and destroys the filtering system. Both elements in this proposition, the robustness of the religion and the political ideology, need careful attention.

First, Islam is built on a vision of special divine revelation whose verbal medium, the Qur'an, cannot be questioned in the slightest degree. The literal divinity and inerrancy of the Qur'an is a basic dogma of Islam; it is not an optional opinion; some may doubt it but none may challenge it. Historical and literary criticism are not fitting in this instance, for the human mind cannot stand in judgment over the Word of God. Hence we are to be in no doubt about access to the divine mind and will. Humanity now knows what God requires. Human opinion and judgment, important as they may be on a host of topics, have been corrected and supplemented by the full, final divine Word that surpasses all other divine revelation.

Second, this special divine revelation must be implemented in every sphere of human existence, including human political existence. All of human life must now operate on the basis of divine law. Divine law by its very nature must trump human law. The state, and not just the individual or assembly of individuals, must now adhere to the law of God as revealed in the Qur'an. We are face to face with a firm political ideology in which there cannot, on pain of disloyalty and of self-contradiction, be a separation between religion and the state.

Note what is not at stake in this proposal. There is here no hierarchy of clergy and laity, of priesthood and politician. There is a complicated division of labor where the division shifts in different configurations, but there is a core commitment to an agreed revelation. Nor is there an official *magisterium* that delivers infallible interpretations of the divine Word. There are, of course (as there will be with any set of texts) traditions of interpretation; and there are deep internal differences on the issue of succession; but these in no way undercut the radical equality that exists within Islam. What is at stake is a religious vision of politics where all are called to serve a common divine mandate.

Furthermore, Islam is not a religious version of communism or fascism. Compared to the basic Islamic vision of politics, communism and fascism are two failed, ephemeral experiments in politics that are now fading into the sunset. No doubt they will linger on for a time; and we can expect that they will be revived and reworked; but they do not begin to match the religious pedigree and heritage of Islam. Nor should we look at this vision in terms of secular imperialisms; these too come and go; Islam with all its changes and developments has outlasted them and operates on radically different foundations. Nor again should we dismiss this vision as another form of Fundamentalism. This is an overused theological swearword that best fits a form of volatile, conservative Christianity in the West whose engagement in politics waxes and wanes across the generations. Moreover, its application to Islam does not begin to do justice to the depth, rigor, and complexity of Islamic faith.

What is at stake in mainstream Islam is both simple and complex. At its core there is a loyalty that transcends all others. Islam is a theocracy in which God is the supreme sovereign. It possesses a theocentric vision of equality and justice that is felt by insiders to be liberating and fulfilling. It upholds a muscular vision of creation and redemption that gives it deep and broad horizons. A simple but profound spirituality undergirds it. By its own logic it creates a brotherhood, a nation of nations, a society that embraces the whole world. This worldwide *ummah* is marked by large gatherings that give a sense of global identity and small meetings that bespeak intimacy. It is open to the most learned scholar and the most illiterate peasant. There is an uncomplicated point of entry and a clear-cut system of demarcation to identify outsiders and unbelievers. The core goals, values, and doctrines of Islam are proclaimed in mosques that can rally the faithful every Friday. These are also reiterated in a network of simple religious practices that express and sustain them on a daily basis. There are myriad educational institutions from elementary schools to universities to teach the faithful. There are vast sums of money to articulate and defend the faith both within and without mainstream educational institutions. There is a cross-cultural body of literature that can be disseminated in schools to expound and explain the principles involved. There is a long tradition of complex jurisprudence on which to draw to work out the details; there is poetry and music to write God's law on the heart and to steady the will. Where Islam is taken seriously, there is a confidence and sense of obligation to spread this vision everywhere. There is also a natural sense of superiority over all religious rivals. There is a hearty no-nonsense attitude to intimidation and insult. There is a readiness when appropriate to use lethal force to defend the faithful, kill apostates, and create favorable conditions for conversion.

We are not speaking here of a tired or dying faith. Islam is a living, breathing religion with a tough political ideology that is supported by historical origination, longstanding continuity, and contemporary models. Its founder did not hesitate to see off his enemies and implement his vision once he moved from Mecca to Medina. Islam spread rapidly eastwards and westwards, creating its own unique political and social world wherever it went. Despite deep internal differences, the common core vision of Islam continues to this day as a live option for political life, as we see across the world from Indonesia to Saudi Arabia. Once mainstream Islam is embraced the separation of religion and politics has come to an end; once Islam is implemented, the filtering system disappears over time.

A Secularist Warrior

In these circumstances it is not surprising that secularists are alarmed. "We are at war with Islam," declares Sam Harris.[47] In fact Harris has hoisted the banner of secularism so high that he has declared war on all religion. The real problem, he insists, is that "every religion preaches the truth of propositions for which it has no evidence. In fact, every religion preaches the truth of propositions for which no evidence is even *conceivable*."[48] Harris displays the same dogmatism, ignorance, and paranoia that one finds in Christian Fundamentalist groups that are already stocking up on weapons and food in preparation for the coming showdown between Islam and the West. Moreover, both Harris and the Fundamentalists have bet their existence on resolving once and for all the problem of the criterion of truth. Fundamentalists, like their Protestant and Catholic forbears, think that if they can only get the right book and then interpret it correctly, they have saved the world. Harris, like some of his strident Enlightenment forbears, thinks that we will save the world if and only if we stick to the narrow criterion of reason reduced to a public appeal to propositional evidence. The latter is in fact a peculiar secularization of the former; the theory of knowledge at work in and around the Reformation has been given a new lease of life in a narrow, evidentialist vision that is unpersuasive, inhuman, and unworkable in practice. Harris' canon of teachers is, of course, very different from that of the Fundamentalists. The Pope in Harris' canon is English; it is the brilliant, oddball philosopher, Bertrand Russell, the inventor and advocate of Logical Atomism. The Pope in the Fundamentalist canon is Irish; it is the ingenious, oddball theologian, John Nelson Derby, the inventor and advocate of Dispensationalism.

In the meantime ordinary people remain worried. They are amused but not surprised at the overreaction to Islam in some religious circles in the West, but they are not amused when they look at the situation as a whole. There are wars and rumors of war. They

[47] Sam Harris, *The End of Faith, Religion, Terror, and the Future of Reason* (New York: W. W. Norton and Company, 2004), 109. I discuss Harris' analysis of the challenge of Islam further in chapter 5.

[48] Ibid., 23, emphasis as in the original.

cannot avoid the conflict and confusion that saturate the media. They know that things are never going to be the same again. They hope that Islam can be assimilated; and they want to cheer on those who are prepared to modify and liberalize it; but they are skeptical that the radical reformers will be the majority report. Nor are they at all sure that they can accept the aggressive secular agenda represented by philosophers like Sam Harris.

A Decent Future Together

The first order of business is to regain a sense of proportion. We need to steady our nerves and face other facets of the situation. We should not get our underwear in a twist simply because a new religion has arrived in the neighborhood. To begin, it is one thing to aspire to establish the political ideology of a worldwide missionary religion as the law of the land; it is another to establish it. There has always been a gap between aspiration and reality, even within Islam itself. Moreover, there is a ceiling to success, as radical Islamists are discovering in Afghanistan, Algeria, and the Sudan. Every religion has its fanatics who want to take over the world; they have never succeeded; their dreams, like those of secular totalitarians end up as nightmares. Also, despite the unity at the core of Islam, the differences are deep and long lasting, stretching right back to the first generation after Muhammad. The sectarian brutality manifest within Islam between Sunni and Shia not only makes Islam abhorrent to many outsiders, it halts the drive to global hegemony. So too does the presence of pietists within Islam who put more store by the internal dimensions of faith than by external obedience.[49] And the effort to make Islam compatible with western notions of tolerance and democracy is not going to roll over and surrender any time soon. Nor is the long, hard-won tradition in the West of distinguishing between church and state going under any day soon. In any case, it is nonsensical to think that Muslim missionaries are going to convert a majority of humanists, communists, atheists, agnostics, Christians, Hindus, Buddhists, and all the other tribes of belief and unbelief across the face of the earth. It is simply false to think that the world is going to be flooded with Islam and its political ideology. Muslim missionaries are not going to be that successful; billions from a host of diverse religions and philosophies

[49]For a gripping account of the journey from radical Islam back to Sufi pietism see Ed Husain, *The Islamist* (London: Penguin, 2007).

are not going either to convert or to accept the political ideology of mainstream Islam.

The second order of business is to keep our intellectual nerve. We should not give in to intellectual paranoia. It helps at this point to revisit the crucial distinction that was made after the wars of religion in Europe. It is one thing to challenge divine revelation; it is another to challenge someone's claim to possess a divine revelation. It is one thing to pit one's fallible, vulnerable mind against God; it is another to ask obvious questions about someone's fallible, vulnerable claim to have possession of divine revelation. When someone claims to possess a divine revelation, it is neither irrational nor blasphemous to ask questions about their claim to possess divine revelation. When we do so we are not challenging God, we are simply asking entirely appropriate questions of one another. To be sure, we may have lost the art of pursuing such questions. Philosophers and theologians entered into a strange alliance in the twentieth century that conspired to dismiss such questions as meaningless or beyond the reach of reason. But we are now in a new day, and we can no longer afford such dogmatism.

My Muslim friend, Farouk, in Katmandu was perfectly willingly to discuss why he believed Islam was the final Word from God. He was committed to the intellectual virtue of rationality; he was open to discussing whether some of his foundational commitments were intellectually legitimate. This disposition opens the door to a whole network of intellectual virtues and practices that are vital to democracy. Currently the jury is out on whether enough Muslims will be like Farouk; some regrettably and tragically have opted for violence. If Muslims are prepared to face the inescapable questions that ordinary people rightly have about the legitimacy of particular claims to possess divine revelation, then we are already on the path to a decent future together.

It helps to compare the problems we face with what has happened in Ireland. Aside from the problem of defeating terrorism, the fundamental problems were constitutional and practical. The crucial sticking points were these. First, how do we gain commitment to resolving disputes by rational rather than violent means? The solution was to secure basic order by the use of lethal force, disarm the terrorist agencies, bring the rival groups into the political arena, and get agreement on the principle of consent in politics. Second, how do we acknowledge the incompatible national aspirations of two groups with roots in rival versions of the Christian religion, who have very different cultural commitments, and yet who occupy the same piece of real estate? The crucial solution involved the recognition of the different cultural traditions (and even languages) and the development of complex institutions that remained rooted in the Westminster parliament in London but which reached across the border to Dublin. Third, how do we get all sides to accept the basic institutions of law and order? The solution was to insist on the public decommissioning of paramilitary weapons and the creation of a new police force that would have exclusive monopoly of lethal power throughout the country. Fourth, how do we prevent a majority party or coalition of parties from imposing their convictions on a minority who believe that such imposition is a denial of vital freedoms? The solution was a complex system of elections and shared governance in which the agreement of minorities was essential to the implementation of political policies. Getting the correct formulae for these arrangements and then implementing them has been fiendishly difficult.

In Ireland we are dealing with a world where the terrorists involved could not and did not help themselves to the warrants of the Christian faith. There was an agreed commitment to the basic presuppositions of liberal democracy. There was sufficient good will to stay the course. Outside agents, like the American Administration and the Dublin government, who wanted to lend a hand, were in broad agreement on what to do. As to the relation between faith and politics, either there was enough agreement across the religious divides to permit progress, or the distinction between church and state was already accepted and workable. So it was possible to work both from the top down from a network of shared rational assumptions and from the bottom up where the differences were carefully negotiated into a messy compromise.

An Open Question to an Open Letter

We do not yet know how Muslims are going to handle the new circumstances in which they now find themselves with the rise of globalization and their encounter with the West. The beginnings of an answer are contained in *A Common Word Between Us and You* which is "An Open Letter and Call from Muslim Religious Leaders to His Holiness Pope Benedict XVI" and a raft of other Christian leaders.[50] The letter begins with a common word that insists that the basis for peace and justice between Christian and Muslims already exists. That common word can be found in the shared commitment to the unity of God, the love of God, and the love of neighbor. So far so good; all people of goodwill will be delighted to receive these opening remarks.

Everything hinges at this point on the small print. It is very clear that in fact there is much less of a common word in the small print than its enthusiastic reception would warrant. As the earlier *Open Letter to His Holiness Pope Benedict XVI* also makes clear, Muslims and Christians do not worship the same God, for the Muslim vision of the unity of God rules out the Christian vision of God as also triune.[51] *A Common Word* reiterates no less than thirteen times in fourteen pages that God has no associate or partner. This is not a throwaway remark; it is an obvious and repeated rejection of the divinity of Christ. Once we come to terms with this crucial quali- fication on the identity of God, the first and second elements of agreement have been undermined. If Christians and Muslims do not worship the same God, then they do not love the same God.

As to love for neighbor, the letter puts the issue clearly. In Islam this injunction is stated as follows: "None of you has faith until you love for your brother what you love for yourself." As it stands this does not at all involve loving the neighbor categorically. The object of love is not the neighbor but what we love for ourselves. No doubt this worry will be dismissed as moral and theological nit-picking; it is nothing of the kind, for everything depends on careful attention to detail. The injunction does not call for love of neighbor categori- cally and unconditionally, rather it enjoins loving for our neighbor what we love for ourselves. This is radically different from loving the neighbor categorically and unconditionally as ourselves.

The importance of this observation surfaces immediately when we turn to the call that is made to Christians.

> In the Holy Qur'an, God Most High tells Muslims to issue the following call to Christians (and Jews—the People of the Scrip- ture): Say: O People of the Scripture! Come to a common word between us and you: that we shall worship none but God, and

[50]The letter can be found and downloaded at http://www.acommonword.com/lib/ downloads/CW-Total-Final-v-12g-Eng-9-10-07.pdf [accessed January 6, 2013].

[51]This letter is available for download here www.ammanmessage.com/media/open- Letter/english.pdf [accessed January 6, 2013].

that we shall ascribe no partner unto Him, and that none shall
take others for lords beside God. And if they turn away, then say;
Bear witness that we are they who have surrendered (unto Him).
(Aal 'Imran 3:64)[52]

This is an astonishing request. Rather than a call to affirm common
beliefs it is nothing less than a call to convert to Islam. However,
this call makes perfect sense when we line it up alongside the injunction to love for our neighbor what we love for ourselves. For
devout Muslims there can be nothing more important in their lives
than serving the one true God; hence to love for the neighbor what
is loved for ourselves will involve coming to serve the one true God
and abandoning the worship and love of Jesus Christ. This is not
a common word shared by Christians, Jews, and Muslims; it is a
particular and unique word that is exclusively Muslim in content.
It is simply and categorically a call to abandon the Christian faith
and convert to Islam.

It is very tempting to hold our tongues at this point and cheer
on Liberal-oriented Muslims in their struggle with the radicals. We
should, of course, welcome every effort to foster peace and justice.
Yet we need to be firm in pressing our questions to mainstream
Muslims. As it stands the common word and call is a sophisticated
exercise in irrelevance that fails to mention the issues that really
matter if we are to have a serious conversation. We need at this stage
a reality check for the future of Islam. Here are the questions that
need to be addressed. Do you or do you not permit conversion to
other religions without any penalties? Do you or do you not consent to robust missionary work by other religions in the Islamic
homelands? Do you or do you not agree to the existence of the state
of Israel? Do you or do you not distinguish clearly between your
religious duties as Muslims and your social and political obligations
in a pluralist society? Do you or do you not distinguish between
religion and politics? Do you or do you not as Muslims privilege
your identity in the *ummah* over your national identity? Do you
or do you not as Muslims require in the end that *sharia* law be the
law of the land? Do you or do you not think that a positive answer
to each of these questions arises out of the core commitments of
devout Muslims? These are not trick questions; they go to the heart

of our religious and political future.

The difficulties we now face in the West as a whole are much greater than those we have faced in Ireland. Bloody wars are afoot with no end in sight. There are terrorists whose killing sprees are grounded in religion. The weapons that can be used are now much more lethal. There are storm clouds of hatred, resentment, and fear. National and international agents are not in agreement on how to proceed. The commitment to liberal democracy is not assured. There are deep and consequential differences on what to do with the toxic effects of religion in the public square. There are problems aplenty that run all the way from the top to the bottom of the political order. The challenge of terrorism will be with us for a very long time.

It is tempting to say that the solution adopted in Ireland was peculiarly Irish. It would be wonderful to hope that in the broader challenges we now face, life might be short, nasty and Irish. The danger is that it will be short, nasty, and brutish.

5

Joes and Josephines

A Mother's Wise Advice

Whenever I underestimated my mother's knowledge, she had a standard, witty reply. She would say: "I may not have gone much to school, but I did meet the scholars coming home." This is an invaluable adage in dealing with terrorism.

Terrorists are intent on killing innocents anywhere. So there is little or no chance of taking evasive action when they attack. Some folk on the planes on 9/11 were fortunate in being able to call loved ones on their cell phones. It is rare to have an opportunity to counterattack, as happened on United Airlines Flight 93 that crashed into a field near the town of Shanksville in rural Somerset County in Pennsylvania. On that flight passengers and members of the flight crew fought courageously to take back the plane from the hijackers. Moreover, terrorists want us to spend our lives in fear; so we are right to resist the fears evoked by terrorism by living life as normally as possible. Folk were offended when President George W. Bush proposed at one point that we should answer the challenge of terrorism after 9/11 by shopping or going to a ballgame; some thought that this trivialized the challenge we faced; others thought he was fostering consumerism as a national addiction; but he had a very valid point. The disruption of normal life is at the heart of terrorist intentions; so living normal lives is certainly one of the best ways to limit their success. In the early years of terrorism in Ireland I certainly resonated with this way of dealing with it. Terrorism was so much of the air we breathed that normal life with its various trials and afflictions was a welcome relief.

Another source of relief was the gallows humor that readily sprung up out of nowhere. Did you hear the one about Gerry Adams and Martin McGuiness when they were rookie terrorist operatives? They were on their way to plant a bomb at the local police station and stopped at a red light. Adams was driving and McGuiness was holding the bomb in his lap in the passenger seat. They had tried valiantly to remember all the details of the training that was supposed to help them stay calm under tension, but this was not working. When they stopped at the red light, McGuiness began to shake and tremble uncontrollably. Like the traffic lights, his color changed from red, to yellow, to green. "What's the matter with you," Adams asked. "Jasus, Mary, and Joseph," said McGuiness, "I am afraid of this bomb going off in my bloody hands." "God help us, you frickin eegit," said Adams, "Don't worry your head about it! Have you forgotten that we have another bomb in the back seat?"

Or did you hear the one about the Rev. Dr. Ian Paisley? He was preaching one Sunday evening in the Free Presbyterian Church in Ballygobackwards. The Free Presbyterian Church, by the way, is neither free nor Presbyterian; it is Free Presbyterian. Paisley was winding up to the climax of his sermon, making it clear what would happen if they did not heed his message. "Let me warn you," he thundered, "if you do not now—immediately—at this very minute—repent of your sins, you are all going to hell. And there, it says so right here in the Infallible Word of God, there you will burn eternally. And there, there will be a weeping and a gnaaashing of teeth. Yes, mark God's holy Word, there will be a weeping and a gnaaashing of teeth!" By this time everyone in the church, even Paisley himself was terrified. Then a wee woman with white hair in the front row piped up and said (in a voice just loud enough for all to hear), "Dr. Paisley, I don't have any teeth!" To which Dr. Paisley instantly replied: "Old woman! You fool! Teeth will be provided!"

Supporting the Cause of Justice

Not everyone will find relief in this kind of humor, but many do. It is very much part of normal life in Ireland. Gallows humor will not help much, of course, when terrorists target civilians who move into professions, like the law, that are a real threat to their activities. Nor will it help when they turn on the loved ones of those who form and lead campaigns to get justice for their family members. Consider two examples.

In the late 1970s, Edgar Graham was a jewel of the legal profession in Belfast. He had studied law at Oxford and returned to Queen's University law faculty as a rising star in academia. He was particularly interested in how the law might be developed to inhibit terrorists and bring them to justice.[53] Born in 1954, at twenty-eight he was also a rising star in the Unionist Party, destined, according to those in the know, to become its leader one day.

On the morning of December 7, 1983, the last day of tutorials, Edgar Graham was chatting with a colleague outside 19 University Square on his way to deliver a lecture there. I knew the street intimately because for four years I had been a student in the philosophy department that was housed a few doors away from the faculty of law. He was shot six times in the head by a young man in a jogging suit, who escaped with a companion by fleeing across the campus. Other plotters ran in all directions to distract witnesses who might otherwise have been able to identify the killers. When the news of his death was announced in the Students' Union building nearby, a loud roar of approval went up from the ranks of the republican students. One of Graham's colleagues on the law faculty, Sylvia Hermon, was there when the news was announced over the public-address system and heard the sickening cheer of victory; she has never been able to set foot in the Union building since then. Sometime earlier she had challenged two strange men in 19 University Square who were intent on reading an examination timetable. She followed them into Botanic Avenue just round the corner where a police officer had intercepted them. When questioned, one of them said he had been checking the timetable for his sister who was reading geography and law, a non-existent combined course. It all sounded suspicious, but they could do nothing. The choice of the university as a place to kill was quite deliberate; the murder sent chills through the whole academic community. The gunmen are still at large today; their identity is well known.[54] On his tombstone Anne Graham, Edgar Graham's sister, chose a quote from Euripides

---

[53] On the American side this issue is taken up by John Yoo in *War by Other Means,: An Insider's Account of the War on Terror* (New York: Atlantic Monthly Press, 2006).

[54] See Dean Godson, *Himself Alone: David Trimble and the Ordeal of Unionism* (London: Harper Collins, 2004), 78.

as part of the epitaph: "Keep alive the light of justice."

Keeping alive the light of justice is a demanding task. Those who are the immediate victims of terrorism can fight back by using all the political, cultural, and legal resources available. Take the extraordinary case of the McCartney sisters, Paula, Gemma, Catherine, Claire, and Donna. The IRA murdered their brother, Robert McCartney, on January 31, 2005. On the night before McCartney had gotten into a fight in Magennis's bar in May Street in the center of Belfast. The fight arose when members of the IRA accused McCartney's friend, Brendan Devine, of making a rude gesture to a group of women in their company. A brawl broke out when Devine refused to apologize. Devine survived, but McCartney was found unconscious with stab wounds in Cromac Street and died in hospital the next day at 8.10 a.m. He had been beaten about the head and legs with sewer rods. His throat had been cut several times, and there was another slashing cut from his chest to his navel. A thousand mourners attended the funeral; the rows of stitches around his neck were so thick that one of the mourners initially thought he was wearing a neck chain. A Catholic, Robert McCartney lived in the nationalist Short Strand area of East Belfast. He was a father of two and engaged to be married to his long-term partner, Bridgeen Hagans, in the summer of 2005.

The clean-up operation afterwards was meticulous. Women members and supporters of the IRA stepped in immediately and expertly scrubbed the crime scene; they used bleach because bleach destroys forensic evidence. The CCTV film was removed and destroyed. The police investigation was met with a wall of silence. Because of intimidation many of the seventy-two witnesses claimed to be otherwise engaged in the pub's two tiny toilets at the time of the attack. The toilets were later dubbed the TARDIS, after the time machine in the series *Doctor Who*, which is much bigger on the inside than on the outside.

The five McCartney sisters and her brother's partner went to work to bring the killers to justice. This was far from easy at the time, for the killing was overshadowed by the robbery of a Northern Bank building in Belfast on December 2004 in which over $50 million was stolen. It is widely believed that the IRA had carried this out. On 8 March 2005 the IRA offered to shoot the perpetrators; the McCartney sisters rejected this incredible offer with the derision it deserved. When their public campaign for justice was in full swing, Martin McGuiness, a leader in Sinn Féin, made a public pronouncement that the sisters should be careful not to be manipulated for political ends. Many saw this as a threat. Yet the McCartney sisters traveled in March 2005 to the United States for the St. Patrick's Day celebrations, where they met Senator Hilary Clinton and President George W. Bush. Even Senator Ted Kennedy shunned Gerry Adams on this occasion. Once out of the spotlight, though, the McCartney family were forced out of their homes in the Short Strand Catholic enclave, where they had lived for five generations. Despite extraordinary opposition, they are staying the course to see the killers brought to justice. On January 31, 2007, Gerry Adams said that anyone with information about the murder should go to the police. On the signing of the agreement between Gerry Adams and Ian Paisley on March 26, 2007, Paisley promised to take the issue up with Adams. Courage and tenacity like this are pivotal in the fight against terrorism.

The kind of activity taken up by Edgar Graham and the McCartney sisters are not serious options for most of us. We are not and will never be eminent lawyers; nor can we see ourselves acting heroically when the terrorists come to kill family members. However, we all know such courageous people, and we can surely do what we can to encourage and support them. Their struggles are often lonely and desolate; we can give them moral support by standing with them in the pursuit of justice. Their work and struggle depends on a multitude of actions by ordinary citizens coordinated through the webs of relationships that exist in society. Edgar Graham, as my mother would have said, did not come up the river in a cabbage head. He was nurtured in a family and in a community that prepared him for his work as a superb young lawyer. With the death of Robert McCartney, the McCartney sisters lost the last male member of their family; they were stalwart supporters of Irish nationalism; yet they found such strength in their bond as a family that they were able to take on the terrorists in their community. They also found support in the thousands of ordinary citizens who cheered them on.

The Importance of State Action

Similar considerations apply to the actions of the state in defeating terrorism. We rightly look to the state to do the heavy lifting in responding to terrorism, but we need to provide support to the state to get the job done. Happily the state has a lot of weapons in its arsenal. It can train special forces and actively pursue terrorists on the ground. It can enforce sanctions on suppliers of nuclear technology to terrorist states. It can impose diplomatic, economic, and military sanctions. By freezing funding, it can neutralize terrorist enclaves that are the breeding ground for terrorists and that serve as proxy terrorists for states. It can freeze financial assets of terrorist regimes and organizations. It can team up with other states to develop a coordinated response at an international level. It can share intelligence, revise legislation to make possible greater surveillance of terrorist organizations, outlaw funding to terrorist groups, investigate groups preaching terror and the violent overthrow of the government, tighten gun control, attend to immigration law, look into the connections between terrorism and organized crime, and so on.[55] However, it is a big mistake to think that the state can work in a vacuum; it needs intelligent, self-critical engagement and support from its ordinary citizens. We can hurt or hinder the state in its work.

As citizens we dare not remain aloof from such matters if we care about responding to terrorism. In a vibrant democracy these decisions can only be taken if there are good politicians in place and if there is both the will and the permission to take appropriate action against terrorism. We need first-rate politicians who can rise above partisan politics and really make smart, effective decisions. Like Edgar Graham, these do not come up the river in a cabbage head; they have to be nurtured, encouraged, educated, and supported. Where we are going to find the next Abraham Lincoln who will have the savvy, temperament, ability, and integrity that is vital in the leadership of a democracy in times of acute crisis? They will arise from within our families, religious groups, and civic organizations, those basic units that provide the soil for competent leadership. This is not rocket science; it is more like providing informal apprenticeships in political proficiency. We need people of will and determination who can see the challenge through to the end, articulate clearly what is going on, and pave the way for their

---

[55] I am indebted for these suggestions to Benjamin Netanyahu, *Fighting Terrorism, How Democracies Can Defeat the International Terrorist Network* (New York: Farrar, Straus and Giroux, 2001), chap. 7. Netanyahu, before his entry into politics, was a member of an elite anti-terror unit in the Israeli Army.

successors. Such leaders will not come from outer space; they will come from within our loins and local communities.

Equally, we need to provide intelligent permission for the kind of state action that will really work without sacrificing our hard-won social principles and values. The debates this will involve are not for the faint-hearted; they are for those who can get beyond the emotional polemic, the grandstanding politician, and the politically partisan activist. The latter can easily breed cynicism and despair, those characteristic enemies of good judgment and political engagement. Cynicism and despair certainly ratchet up the realism quotient by making us come to terms with the incompetence and stupidity of our leaders and with the worst that can befall us. However, they are no substitute for the steady hand and head that we surely need. No modern democratic state can operate effectively in the war on terror without the permission of its people. The formal and informal media hammer away at the issues relentlessly; elections send very clear signals; public opinion polls are factored into state decisions on a regular basis. These practices are not some sinister plot invented to ruin our lives; they are the messy mechanisms that register our preferences and provide the wider context for state action; they are our informal intelligence service. We should welcome their interest in recording our two cents worth of wisdom, will and judgment and we should be willing to supply them with it.

Certainly we can choose to do nothing. Nobody will get on our case if we take this option. However, the choices are not confined to great acts of heroism or doing nothing at all. It is not as if, as one of my friends playfully suggested, we should all go off and take a martial arts course before we step on the next airplane, so that we will be ready to take on any terrorists that might be on board. As ordinary citizens what we need is not some grand program to defeat terrorism; we simply need to attend a little more actively to what we already do. If everybody puts his or her penny on the plate, the final count will surprise us.

Our response to terrorism surely means doing more than simply rearing our families and having our views picked up here and there by the media. We can become active agents within the political arena. Terrorism is a political practice. As with counterfeit money, the best way to drive out bad money is to make sure that there is plenty of good money available. The conventional practices of democracy are both banal and boisterous. The political process is incredibly slow, tedious, demonizing, and never-ending. Marxists have dismissed representative democracy as manipulated by the rich to devour the poor; fascists have rejected it because it lacks blood and thunder in times of crisis. The whole of the twentieth century was one long battle with communists and fascists who set out to undermine representative democracy as a viable way of making decisions and living together. If we lived in an ideal world, it is unlikely that we would adopt representative democracy as the best way to organize society. From the days of Plato, folk have had their doubts about it. Terrorism shows us how precious representative democracy is. The alternatives promise freedom and deliver death. Islamist radicals now oppose democracy because they see it as a jungle of ignorance let loose against the law of God as revealed in the Qur'an through their favored interpreters. Once again this fragile form of organizing society is on the line. Terrorism sharply concentrates the mind by showing that there is another political practice to ponder. Do we want terrorism as the political practice of choice; or do we want to pump new life into the banal and boisterous practices of democracy? I vote we vote.

Central to voting is becoming an informed citizen. The resources on terrorism currently available are rich and varied: television dramas and documentaries, magazine articles, newspaper coverage, fiction, non-fiction books galore, and, of course, the internet.[56] If we were to give as much attention to reading around the topic of terrorism as we do, say, to reading around the latest fashion craze, or around our favored sport, we would find ourselves readily equipped to map the terrain. Suppose we gave the same attention that some give to the Final Four tournament in college basketball during March Madness, or that others give to the draft for the NFL. There really is no excuse. If terrorists can find the time to read manuals and search the internet, we ought to find the time to read a few good books on terrorism and search the internet ourselves. While we should consult the experts on relevant dimensions of ter-

---

[56]Here is a small sample of varied recent texts: Bruce Hoffman, *Inside Terrorism* (New York: Columbia University Press, 2006), revised edition; Mary R. Habeck, *Knowing the Enemy* (New York: Yale University Press, 2006); John Updike, *Terrorist* (New York: Alfred A. Knopf, 2006); Seyyed Vali Reza Nasr, *The Shia Revival* (New York: Norton, 2006); Brigitte Gabriel, *Because They Hate* (New York: St. Martin's Press, 2006).

rorism, there is a sense in which everybody is a layperson. The topic is vast, there are many dimensions to it, but we can dig in where it catches our imagination and interests. Of course it will take time to get our bearings, but we cannot afford not to do this. The lives of our children and grandchildren are at stake.

In educating ourselves, we will no doubt need to be ready to venture into new territory and to break through barriers that have been erected to keep us from probing too deeply. Intellectual fences will have to be broken and new boundaries of inquiry established. The topic can be a depressing one. There are no neutral observers. Political commitments will protrude and raise the temperature. Multiculturalism has intimidated us from serious evaluation of minority opinions and ideologies. It will be easy to get into arguments with friends and colleagues at Starbucks. Staying cool and keeping one's mouth shut will really matter at times. However, the knowledge gained is power. It will put our fears in perspective, and it will foster the will to act in an effective way within the options open to us.

Find Out the Facts

A test case is in my own self-education in terrorism. I set out to answer two factual questions that are obviously important. First, is it likely that there are suitcase nuclear bombs out there in the hands of terrorists? Second, is it likely that there are sleeper cells of Islamic terrorists in the United States? I set myself three rules. I would give myself a weekend to find out, I would not consult the mini-library of books I already had in hand, and I would not search the internet. So I made a quick visit to the terrorism section of my local *Half-Price* bookstore and a second visit to one of my favorite mainline bookstores round the corner. Here are the results of my findings.

Take the suitcase nuke question first. Is it likely that there are suitcase nuclear bombs out there in the hands of terrorists? We know that al-Qaeda has been intent on finding nuclear weapons and using them against the United States. The most chilling evidence for this is the fatwā that bin Laden sought and received from Shaykh Nasir bin Hamid al-Fadh in May 2003. The fatwā was entitled: "A treatise on the legal status of using Weapons of Mass Destruction against infidels." It concludes: "If a bomb that killed ten million of them and burned as much of their land as they have burned

Muslim's land were dropped on them, it would be permissible."[57] With this in mind, it is not difficult to jump to the conclusion that sooner or later we are in for a nuclear strike. Not surprisingly, a leading newspaper, the *Boston Globe*, in a December 2001 article, speculated that terrorists would explode suitcase nukes in Chicago, Sydney, and Jerusalem in 2004. We now know, of course, that this speculation turned out to be false.

The source of the suitcase nuclear option is the Russian General Alexander Lebed. He told both a U.S. congressional delegation to Moscow in 1997 and the CBS series *60 Minutes* that a number of Soviet-era nuclear suitcase bombs were missing. This was taken up a notch when Colonel Stanislav Lunev, a very high-ranking Soviet defector, told a congressional panel that same year that Soviet Special Forces might have smuggled a number of portable nuclear bombs onto the mainland to be detonated if the cold war got too hot. Then in 2004 a Harvard professor, Graham Allison, wrote a book expressing deep worries about stolen warheads, self-made bombs, and suitcase nukes.[58] My temperature started to rise: al-Qaeda is clearly intent on using nuclear weapons, they have the will to do so, and there are suitcase nukes out there in no-man's-land. Surely, they must have a suitcase bomb.

However, all this was premature. General Lebed was unreliable in his testimony. His numbers kept changing; and he admitted that he did not have time to find out how many such weapons there were. He had never visited the relevant facilities, and he had a history of telling lies. Colonel Lunev's testimony was also deeply flawed. It turns out that his work was to find drop sites for the bombs; he had never actually seen any suitcase nukes. Furthermore, claims about the size and firing of the weapon (that it would take a 60 x 40 x 20 centimeter case and that one person can detonate it) were simply false. The only public person ever to admit to having seen a suitcase-size nuclear device is Rose Gottemoeller, a Defense Department official. She had monitored compliance with disarmament treatises in the early 1990s. The weapon she saw was the size of three footlockers, and it required a team of several people to detonate. In addition, Lebed's deputy, Vladimir Denisov, after a

---

[57] Quoted in Richard Miniter, *Disinformation* (Washinton, D.C.: Regnery, 2005), 137.
[58] Graham Allison, *Nuclear Weapons: The Ultimate Preventable Catastrophe* (New York: Times Books/Holt, 2004).

special investigation conducted before Lebed made his claims, insisted that no army field units had portable nuclear weapons. In fact all portable nuclear devices were stored in a central facility under heavy guard. Lieutenant General Igor Valynkin, chief of the Russian Defense Ministry's 12th Main Directorate, corroborated this by testifying that no nuclear weapons were missing. He also insisted that as a matter of physics and engineering the nuclear suitcase, while technically possible, would be an impractical weapon. The radioactive material used would decay in a few months and would be too costly to maintain; a suitcase nuke would require a lot of shielding. As to the 300 Special Atomic Demolition Munitions (measuring 34 x 26 x 26 inches and weighing 154 lbs) developed by the Americans, all these were dismantled and disposed of in accordance with the unilateral disarmament initiatives of 1991 and 1992.

Moreover, the evidence for claims that al-Qaeda may have bought, stolen, or made nuclear weapons is extremely thin. In fact, al-Qaeda has been taken for a ride, losing in one instance $1.5 million that was forked out for a three-foot-long metal canister with South African markings. The material may have been taken from the innards of an x-ray machine. Furthermore, known thefts of highly enriched uranium between 1994 and 2004 were so low in quantity and poor in quality that even when combined they would not have been enough to make a suitcase nuke. As to making a bomb from scratch, there is no evidence that al-Qaeda is anywhere near succeeding. So the conclusion I reached by Monday morning was this: al-Qaeda has the will to find or to make a suitcase nuke; but to date it has not found the way. So my answer to the first question is this: it is highly unlikely that there is a suitcase nuke out there.

What about my second question? Is it likely that there are sleeper cells of Islamic terrorists in the United States? It would be easy to lose our bearings on this one. The country is so vast, the hiding places so numerous, and the tactics sufficiently so ingenious, that getting a fix on any precise answer seems virtually impossible. Al-Qaeda, for example, is like a food franchise; it allows its members to organize and take the initiative on the ground; so there is no centralized body of data that can be identified and mined. Its headquarters may well be buried somewhere in caves in Pakistan and Afghanistan. Even then, terrorist cells are often organized in such a way that penetration is extremely difficult. And even penetration is of limited value because the members are very restricted in what they know about other members and cells. Cell members themselves are trained to blend in to the native environment they plan to attack; so there is little that can be done to detect them. However, we are being much too pessimistic as we begin our search.

The presumption in this instance has to be that there are terrorist cells in the United States. After all, there was a lethal cell in place that carried out the destruction of 9/11. In this instance my inquiries quickly took me on the trail of the Lebanese Islamist group, Hezbollah. Until 9/11 this terrorist group had killed more U.S. citizens than any other radical Islamist group. Located in Lebanon and heavily sponsored by Iran and Syria, Hezbollah is one of the most sophisticated groups intellectually and militarily within radical Islam. It has been highly effective in developing the art of suicide bombing (imported from Iran) and has worked out a clever combination of political engagement, charity work, and terrorism in its public life. Its charismatic leader, Sheik Hassan Naserallah, is very clearly committed to making the United States suffer for the war in Iraq that dislodged Saddam Hussein. His slogan is simple: "Death to America!" Hezbollah has at least 50,000 members and millions of supporters in the Muslim world. It has intelligence operatives trained to a level of skill rivaling that of professional Western intelligence organizations. Its political theology has been brilliantly worked out in detail.[59] It is intent on bringing down the government of Lebanon and installing an Islamic regime modeled on Iran. Both Syria and Iran have been keen to develop a missile earmarked for delivery to them. Both gave much needed military support in the surprise humiliation of the Israeli attacks in the Fall of 2006.

Hezbollah is at work on four continents. One area of special interest is Argentina, in the Tri-border area below the tropic of Capricorn where Argentina, Paraguay, and Bolivia come together. The area is marked by general lawlessness and corruption, with 30,000 émigrés from the Middle East. From there Hezbollah operatives have launched devastating attacks on two Jewish communities. On March 17, 1992, at 3:00 p.m. they blew up the Israeli embassy in Buenos Aires. A Ford F-100 truck, loaded with 220 pounds of

[59]See, for example, Naim Qassem, *Hizbullah (Hezbollah): The Story from Within* (London: Saqui, 2005).

Semtex plastic explosive, drove into the front of the embassy in the downtown area. Materials and body parts were strewn for hundreds of yards around. A Catholic Church and its attached school were also destroyed. Twenty-nine people were killed and more than 220 wounded. Flying glass lacerated more than a dozen children from the Catholic school. On July 18, 1994, at 9:53 a.m. Hezbollah terrorists struck again in Buenos Aires, using a suicide truck bomb to kill 85 and injure more than 240 when they destroyed the AMIA (the Asociación Mutualista Israelita Argentia) building. The building housed social service agencies where elderly Jews picked up their pensions. It was also the headquarters of the chief rabbinate, contained hundreds of thousands of rare Yiddish books rescued from Russia, and was the home of the entire historical records of the Jewish community in Argentina.

This kind of operation is portable to other parts of the world, and not least to the United States. The most surprising location of choice was Charlotte, North Carolina. We know this because of the trial of the Charlotte Hezbollah cell that began on May 23, 2002. The ringleader, Mohammed Hammoud, was from Lebanon. His mentors chose Charlotte because law enforcement agents were likely to be inexperienced in anti-terrorism surveillance. Moreover, the police were preoccupied with drug wars and motorcycle gangs. In the late eighties and early nineties the city was head over heels in growth. There were direct flights to London and Frankfurt; sixty-nine new foreign enterprises moved into the area between 1989 and 1992. People had gotten used to the presence of foreigners in its midst.

Hammoud's job was to develop a functioning support cell from among the Hezbollah sympathizers within the small Muslim community. Relying on the Shiite doctrine of temporary marriage (*mut'a*) and dissimulation (*taqiyya*) Hammoud built up a small group that was up to its eyeballs in cigarette smuggling, phony marriages, immigration scams, money laundering, and credit fraud. He regularly sent back money to Hezbollah in Lebanon. He even managed to get help from the U.S. Small Business Administration to buy a gas station with his third wife, a charming Greek American with a seductive smile and a flare for crime, Angela Tsioumas. He made one crucial mistake, however, when he recruited Said Mohammed Harb to the cause. When the authorities infiltrated the cell and got on to what Hammoud was up to, Harb was so deep in crime and so unstable that he turned in his comrades. Harb did a deal in which a dozen members of his family were secretly extracted from Lebanon. He was sentenced to three and a half years of imprisonment, but set free because of the time already spent in jail and the usual reductions for good behavior. Hammoud was sentenced to 150 years in prison; he is currently in a federal maximum-security prison in Texas.

So what can we say about Hezbollah cells in the United States more generally? Here is a summary of what I found.

> Besides Charlotte and Dearborn, according to investigators and documents, Hezzbollah supporters are actively involved in criminal conspiracies in New York City; Newark, New Jersey; Boston; Chicago; San Francisco; Louisville; Houston; the Miami-Fort Lauderdale metropolitan area; Los Angeles; Portland, Oregon; Atlanta, Georgia, and Tampa, Florida. Smaller and less organized clusters of sympathizers and fund-raisers are active in scores of other communities throughout the United States.[60]

So the answer to my second question is: yes, there are sleeper cells in the United States.

My weekend of research makes it abundantly clear what can be done by the ordinary layperson that sets out to answer some of the basic factual questions that are essential to being an informed voter. The conclusions are, of course, provisional; there is no claim to finality or infallibility. Indeed this is by no means my own final word on the issue; my aim is simply to press home the need to be focused and disciplined in the effort to find out what is going on; I now have a marker that can be moved in the light of new information. Our provisional findings give a base from which we can then go on to make adjustments as we continue to keep an eye out for relevant information. It also helps in developing the kind of judgment on whom and what to trust when sifting items in the news and the media generally.

Two Stances from Stanford

We are not entitled to our own facts on terrorism, but we are, of course, entitled to our own opinions on the wider questions that swirl around it. Take, for example, the Second Gulf War in Iraq that began on March 20, 2003. The debate on its legitimacy, its tactics,

[60]Tom Diaz and Barbara Newman, *Lightening Out of Lebanon: Hezbollah Terrorists on American Soil* (New York: Ballantine Books, 2005), 229.

and its consequences will rightly continue for years to come. My dog is currently taking a rest from this fight. My dog is interested, however, in another one that is in the neighborhood. How should we tackle the wider question of vital importance, namely, what is the place of mainstream Islam in the battle against terrorism in the West? There are at least three schools of thought worth exploring. Some say that mainstream Islam is the problem, and we should face up to this aggressively. Some say that mainstream Islam is an ally, and that it should be supported to the full in its efforts to marginalize the radicals in Islam. Some say that there are severe challenges up ahead, that the jury is out on this question, and that we should calmly wait and see. The first will detain us for a moment; the other two can be articulated more quickly.

Few have been more ferocious in the attack on Islam than Sam Harris, a Stanford graduate who has a doctorate in cognitive neuroscience.[61] For Harris,

> we are at war with Islam…It is not merely that we are at war with an otherwise peaceful religion that has been "hijacked" by extremists. We are at war with precisely the vision of life that is prescribed to all Muslims in the Koran and further elaborated in the literature of the hadith, which recounts the sayings of the Prophet.[62]

For Harris there are no distinctions between Radical Islam, Mainstream Islam, and Reform Islam. This is not surprising in that he cannot make serious distinctions between Christianity, Judaism, and Islam in that all are a matter of irrational belief from beginning to end. They are all committed to beliefs about the world that float free from reason and evidence. Moderates in religion are nothing more than failed Fundamentalists. The entire project of religion is perfectly backward because it has no evidence in the present to support it; worse still, "every religion preaches the truth of propositions for which no evidence is even *conceivable*."[63] Religious belief is always a matter of a leap of faith and a misuse of the power of our minds. Beliefs like this bring out the worst in us, for religious beliefs are sanctified by faith; hence the wars within and between religions. Religions are black holes that are draining the light from

[61] See Sam Harris, *The End of Faith: Religion, Terror, and The Future of Reason* (New York: W.W. Norton & Co., 2008), chap. 4.

[62] Ibid., 109.

[63] Ibid., 23. Emphasis as in the original.

our world. They arise and are sustained because our fear of death. Faith is "little more than the shadow cast by our hope for a better life beyond the grave."[64]

Islam, Harris goes on, is one rung lower than other religions in the scale of harm because Islam has more than its fair share of bad beliefs. Muslims are Fundamentalists who believe that the Qur'an is the literal and inerrant word of the one true God. They give three, and only three, nasty options to infidels: convert, be subjugated, or be killed. Their views on the relation between religion and the state are incompatible with Western liberalism. They are committed to jihad, holy war, and to world conquest. They are a menace to Jews, because life for the Jews in the House of Islam "has been characterized by ceaseless humiliation and regular pogroms."[65] While Muslims appear tolerant for the moment in the West, this is not the same as genuine liberalism. After all, the penalty for apostasy in Islam is death. In addition, Islam has no resources for avoiding sympathy with the actions of Osama bin Laden. The Qur'an has hosts of passages that show no compassion for those who reject its teaching as divine. In fact, Islam as a whole "has all the markings of a thoroughgoing cult of death."[66] A Pew global survey shows that countries that have Islamic majorities have a striking tolerance of suicide bombing in defense of Islam. To crown it all, the theology of Islam suggests that "the most sexually repressive people found in the world...are lured to martyrdom by a conception of paradise that resembles nothing so much as an al fresco bordello."[67]

The evil that has reached our shores with the arrival of Islam, says Harris, is not merely the evil of terrorism, "it is the evil of religious faith at the moment of its political ascendancy."[68] Once Muslims are in power, they will curtail our freedoms. For them, democracy would simply be a gangplank to theocracy and the introduction of *sharia* law, as it would be in the Islamic strongholds of the world. Liberals who ignore this are simply in denial. Secularists who think that religion is always secondary to politics have gotten it back to front: it is religion that is driving the political and terrorist practices

---

[64] Ibid., 39.
[65] Ibid., 114.
[66] Ibid., 123.
[67] Ibid., 127.
[68] Ibid., 130.

of Islam. They are equally mistaken to think that Muslims are really susceptible to the siren song of Liberalism, or that the real problem lies with the American misdeeds, terrible as these have been over the years. The real problem lies at the core of the Islam itself. Over the years it has failed to develop the moral wealth critical to the treatment of women and children, to the civilized prosecution of war, and to proper criminal justice. "Any systematic approach to ethics, or to understanding the necessary underpinnings of a civil society, will find many Muslims standing eye deep in the red barbarity of the fourteenth century."[69]

If civil society is to survive in these circumstances, argues Harris, we clearly need a counteroffensive to facilitate the emergence of civil societies everywhere. For some Islamic societies this may entail an interim form of benign dictatorship imposed from without. The means to attain this are crude: economic isolation, military intervention (open or covert), or some combination of both. We have no alternative. Of course, such actions will also entail something like a world government, far off as that may seem to most, for otherwise we will not have the public warrants for appropriate intervention. In addition Islam will have to undergo a radical transformation in which the leaders and theologians reshape their religion into an ideology that is basically benign. In the meantime we can apply pressure to the Muslim world by developing alternative energy technologies, a task that should become the object of a new Manhattan Project. If none of this works, we will simply have to "protect our interests with force—continually."[70]

Another Stanford scholar, this time at the Hoover Institution, has taken a radically different line on how to respond to mainstream Islam. Dinesh D'Souza thinks that it is not mainstream Islam but the cultural left in America that is the problem.[71] Over the years self-styled progressives have poisoned Western society by corrupting it from within. Abortionists, feminists, multiculturalists, and homosexual activists have fostered a decadent culture that is morally depraved. In turn this has confirmed Muslims in their worst prejudices against America and evoked a violent response from

---

[69] Ibid., 145.

[70] Ibid., 152.

[71] Dinesh D'Souza, *The Enemy at Home: The Cultural Left and its Responsibility for 9/11* (New York: Doubleday, 2007). D'Souza has since moved on from Stanford to become the President of King's College, New York City.

radical Islamists who see in Western liberalism nothing but an assault on their most cherished values. Radical Muslims have unleashed a crusade that is totalitarian and fascist in order to defend themselves against the enemy. However, radical Muslims are to be distinguished from mainstream Muslims. The latter share the core values of the Judeo-Christian tradition that has been the foundation of western societies. So we should create a wedge between Islamic radicals and traditional Muslims. Traditional Muslims should be welcomed as allies in the opposition to the sensuality, materialism, and corruption that is killing our culture from within. We need a new coalition of moderate Muslims and right-wing conservatives who will come together politically on the shared common ground of traditional values in order to defeat the forces of barbarism (liberal morality) in our midst.

A Third Alternative

Neither of these alternatives strike me as the least persuasive. Harris needs extensive remedial work in the philosophy of religion; his inability to distinguish between different strands of Islam is inexcusable; and his practical suggestions are laughable. D'Sousa proposals, on the other hand, are driven by hatred of progressives; they are the rumblings of a skillful debater; and they are much too naïve in their take on the challenge that mainstream Islam poses to the foundations of representative democracy in the West. So I want to suggest a third way to think about the issue. It is less glamorous and simple than the alternatives. It can be stated by way of two predictions.

First, like all new minorities in the West, we can expect that Muslims will do all they can to find their place in the sun. This will begin with challenging the establishment, using the values of the West to privilege their interests above others, and going after anything that smells of stereotyping and exclusion. We can expect that they will demand accommodation through the courts that will honor their holidays, prayers, beards, and modesty in dress. They will demand respect for their faith from all and sundry. Alongside this they will work their way into the political halls of power in elections. Those who are missionary minded will go further: they will see these moves as a platform for the ultimate conversion of the West, as it collapses from within from the weight of its own decadence and is drawn to Islam by its intrinsic beauty. In anticipation they will press for the introduction of *sharia* law wherever they can. Some Muslims will go further and take on the West in a showdown of sporadic violence that can be contained but will be very difficult to eradicate.

Second, the western democracies will fitfully adjust to the radical changes that the presence of Islam enjoins. These adjustments will be messy and incoherent. Assimilation in the United States will be much more robust than it is in Europe. Muslim enclaves will not be paid for by the state through public housing; Muslims will enter more widely into the job market; radical Muslim clerics will be suppressed; and the verbal virulence of political culture in the United States will ensure that the privileges naturally sought by minorities in the public sphere will not go unchecked. Furthermore, the much greater market of ideas, represented, for example, by a host of competing media outlets, will ensure that the ordinary citizen will be well informed, inspired, and urged to protect the freedoms and practices that are central to a healthy democracy. In addition, the theological and spiritual strength of the Christian and Jewish traditions will ensure that radical forms of both Islam and of secularism will be aggressively confronted intellectually and politically.

The upshot is this. The jury is out at this point in time on how far mainstream Islam will adjust in its entry into the West and on how the West will adjust to its new visitors. The challenge is a real one. It is not at all clear to me how Islam can find the theological and political resources to accept the distinction between religion and politics without which the West simply collapses into a theocracy or into a covert form of confessional atheism. I think, however, that there are enough anti-virus mechanisms deep in the hard drive of the system to keep both at bay. We should keep our heads until all the evidence is in. We should watch the situation in Europe.[72] Even if the worst befalls Europe, as many intelligent observers fear, it is silly to think that this fate awaits the rest of the world. This was the song that was sung in the sixties about the inevitability of secularization and the end of the religion that I was brought up on. It has turned out to be hopelessly wrong, as the arrival of Islam and the resurgence of Christianity in the Third world make patently clear. So we should not see either the United States or the rest of the world

[72]Melanie Phillips, *Londinistan* (New York: Encounter Books, 2006) is indispensable reading here.

as the lapdogs of Europe, waiting with bated breath to see where it goes and then scurrying shamelessly to imitate it.

Staying on Message

What then can the ordinary Joe and Josephine do in responding to terrorism? We can go to the ballgame or head for the mall, living life as normally as possible. We can stand with those brave souls who through the legal profession or through pavement politics keep alive the light of justice. We can raise up and form a new generation of politicians who will be street smart and effective. We can speak up and support our governments in the actions that are essential to protect us from terrorists at home and abroad. We can rediscover and recommit ourselves to the hard-won principles and practices of representative democracy. We can get up off the sofa and become informed voters. We can get answers to the factual questions that need attention. There are no nuclear suitcase bombs floating around; but there are sleeper cells. And we can work on the big picture, looking realistically and patiently at the options that lie before us as an ancient, aggressive, missionary faith finds a home in our neighborhoods and culture.

My mother was right. Even if we do not get much help on terrorism at school, we can still meet the scholars on the way home and learn enough to re-own and preserve the messy but indispensable practices of democratic freedom.

6

The War on Terror

Help on Hand

If terrorists come knocking down my door, I want to have soldiers and a helicopter nearby.

The most famous student during my time at Queens' University, Belfast, in the late sixties was Bernadette Devlin (later Bernadette Devlin McAliskey). She entered as a student in 1965 in Celtic Studies and a year later transferred to the psychology department, where I was also a student at the time, although I scarcely ever saw her. A fiery orator in the civil rights movement of the late sixties, she went on to fame when, in 1969, she was elected the youngest member of the Westminster Parliament in London. Initially she was a convinced Irish Republican, gradually became a socialist, and then combined the two. She became a republican socialist, engaged in a lifetime struggle with "imperialist" Britain from her days in the standard Marxist flag-bearer at Queen's, the "People's Democracy." Her ultimate goal was to create an independent, sovereign, free, and socialist Ireland. Her strategic and tactical views on how to achieve this put her at odds over time with traditional nationalist groups and their leaders. In 1974 she helped form the Irish Republican Socialist Party, a breakaway group from the Official Sinn Féin with connections to the Irish National Liberation Army, in turn a secession from the Official Irish Republican Army. In 1976 she broke with the Irish Republican Socialist Party because it subordinated political activity to military activity and joined the Independent

Socialist Party that disbanded the following year. Much of her early political career was spent within earshot of terrorism; in her later career she has become an articulate commentator and activist at the margins of Northern Irish politics. On February 21, 2003, she was deported from Chicago on her way to a Christening on the grounds that she posed a serious threat to the security of the United States.

Around 8.15 a.m. on Friday, January 16, 1981, Bernadette Devlin McAliskey and her family were the targets of a terrorist attack. At least three loyalist gunmen tore out the phone lines to her country home near the town of Coalisland, used sledgehammers to break down the front door, and opened fire, hitting her in the chest, arm, and thigh. They went on to shoot her husband in the kitchen; their three children were not harmed. It so happened that a patrol of the Third Parachute Regiment was in the area at the time, heard the shots, and rushed to the house. While some of the patrol gave the wounded couple first aid, one of the soldiers ran to a neighbor's house, commandeered a car, and drove to another home to telephone for help. In time a helicopter airlifted the wounded McAliskeys first to a hospital in Dungannon and then to the intensive care facilities at Musgrave Park Hospital in Belfast. Three men were arrested immediately and later charged with a series of terrorist crimes. On the same day three terrorists planted three bombs in the Gables Restaurant in Botanic Avenue, Belfast, and reduced it to rubble; elsewhere two terrorists picked Ivan Tombs out of a line-up of the staff at the Customs Office in Warrenpoint and shot him dead before escaping on a motorcycle.

While the McAliskeys have scorned showing the least shred of gratitude for the extraordinary help provided by the Third Parachute Regiment, without that help they might well have died. This is by no means a unique situation. The first line of defense for anyone threatened by terrorists is the state; even for those who are resolutely opposed to the existence of the state, this is surely the case. The immediate challenge after a terrorist attack is to attend to the dead and wounded, whatever their political or religious identity. For that we need sophisticated agents trained and paid for by the state: law enforcement, ambulance services, medical personnel, fire fighters, intelligence specialists, bomb-disposal experts, and a host of other government employees. Even those who complain of state-terrorism will agree to this elementary empirical observation. To be sure, once we equip the state with lethal power, then there is always the danger that those who act in and for the state will use such power for political ends and thus fall within our concept of terrorism. When this happens we cannot appeal to state power; it is the state itself that is engaging in terrorism.

It was worry about various forms of state terrorism that fuelled the rage and activism of Bernadette Devlin as a student. Beginning with elements of her upbringing that stressed the moral rather than ritualistic side of her Catholicism, she eventually embraced socialism as the political expression of her religious faith. There were times when she was very tempted to engage in violence against the state, but she initially tried the way of non-violence in the civil rights movement. After her election to the Westminster parliament she quickly recognized that she did not have the patience or skill to engage in the compromises of regular democratic politics. Her hopelessly abrasive style that went all the way back to her childhood in a family fraught with fights and resentments only made matters worse.[73] Like many in the late sixties she then pinned her hopes on a socialist revolution that, as applied to Ireland, would bring the working class of both Protestant and Catholic communities together in the creation of whole New Ireland, North and South. Not surprisingly this was utterly rejected on all sides. It involved a naïve assessment of the situation that ignored the strength of nationalist and religious commitments; it also totally underestimated the ingenuity of regular politicians in Ireland and Britain.

In the end she has come to admit defeat. She believes that in the carefully manipulated Peace Process the British and Irish Establishments have outwitted the leadership of Sinn Féin once again. Irish nationalism and British imperialism have worked together to submerge the ideology of republicanism.

> The republican ideology has been abandoned for constitutional, nationalist all-class alliances. And every time that it has happened, it has benefited the greedy who aren't the members of Sinn Féin—they're the members of Fianna Fáil, they're the members of the unionist party, they're the members of the national bourgeoisie of Ireland. Every single time that this new alliance has been created, the people who have suffered have been the poor in Ireland. The dissidents in Ireland. The radicals in Ireland.

[73] See the searing account of her childhood in Bernadette Devlin, *The Price of My Soul* (New York: Random House, 1969).

The women in Ireland. And at every single point, this kind of politics has been bad for the people who have always mattered [to us]—bad for the people that mattered to the leadership of Sinn Féin, and bad for republican politics—bad for republicanism.[74]

In the last analysis, the capacity to create an independent, sovereign, free and socialist Ireland has been undermined. The struggle for equality, human rights, the working class, and socialism has been arrested; it is time, she thinks, to go back again to the drawing board of socialist politics.

It is interesting that Bernadette Devlin McAliskey nowhere mentions liberation theology as an option in her journey. Clearly this would have fitted nicely with her Catholic background, her opposition to imperialism, colonialism, and capitalism, her skepticism about parliamentary democracy, and her enthusiasm for a revised version of Marxism. It would also have given her a whole new angle on terrorism.

The Illusions of Liberation Theology

The core of liberation theology is to look to the story of the poor and marginalized to provide guidance on how to respond to social and political problems.[75] In the Irish situation this story is radically different from those supplied by the rival nationalist groups, for these latter stories are ultimately stories of dominance. They maintain the fabric and morale of the group and their institutions, and they shape the identity of and response to outsiders. While they draw on biblical images and on rival confessional histories, liberation theologians are convinced that they fail to capture the real issues at stake. The real issues at stake are economic and need to be analyzed in terms of class. In the judgment of the Irish Presbyterian theologian, Terence P. McCaughey, British administrations are mistaken to see paramilitary organizations as the root of the disease. These nasty groups are simply symptoms of "a disease somewhere near the real root cause of which is their own stubborn neo-colonial presence in the island..."[76] This causal insight is readily visible to

[74]See Bernadette Devlin McAliskey, "The Peace Process is...,"http://irelandsown.net/McAliskeySpeech.html [accessed 02/26/2007]

[75]The case for this has been made especially well by Joerg Rieger, *Remember the Poor* (Harrisburg: Trinity Press International, 1998).

[76]Terence P. McCaughey, *Memory and Redemption: Church, Politics and Prophetic Redemption in Ireland* (Dublin: Gill and MacMillan, 1993), 59.

the poor. Thus over two hundred years ago Jemmy Hope, a poor weaver from Templepatrick, "offered what may well be the most penetrating analysis of what went wrong."[77] Jemmy Hope insisted that the condition of the laboring class was the fundamental question at issue. Given this account of the problem, the solution is to follow the lead of Ireland's own homegrown socialist, James Connolly, and join in solidarity with the poor and the oppressed, challenging the consumerist free market economy, insisting on genuine neutrality that really opts out of the Western military alliance, and pursuing educational policies that make first-class education available to more than the affluent. In the latter instance,

> Much more important than ensuring that there is a crucifix on the wall of the school assembly hall is to ensure that those who pass by through the school discern the crucifixion at the heart of the society in which they are growing up. At its best, Christian involvement in education has been the believing community's response to the voice of the unheard as they cry out to be liberated from enslavement.[78]

McCaughey's appeal to liberation theology is no more helpful in responding to the problem of terrorism in Ireland than it is in responding to what happened in New York on 9/11. First, it is obvious that in both cases the agency of the terrorists is buried within a network of Marxist or quasi-Marxist causal categories that are unpersuasive and misleading. It is these obsolete categories, which have themselves been used *ad nauseam* to underwrite brutal forms of state terrorism, that do the heavy lifting by way of explanation; religious categories are left behind in the dressing room. No doubt this is one reason why they do not show up in the proposals of Bernadette Devlin McAliskey; for her religion supplies at best a moral starting point for sympathy with the oppressed and the poor. The real causal factors are economic; and the lead agents in this world are capitalists, imperialists, and colonialists (which, being properly translated, means late Imperial Britain and its successor empire, the United States of America). Terrorists in their radical particularity are first submerged and then quietly drowned; they are not taken seriously as primary actors and agents. Second, it is no doubt touching to appeal to the grandiose insights of a fifteen year old, semi-illiterate weaver from Templepatrick as representa-

[77] Ibid., 124.
[78] Ibid., 97.

tive of the poor of his day, but it is daft to trust that he gets his political and economic sums right. Jemmy Hope may have heard that Thomas Paine's *Rights of Man* came to be known by the late 1790s as "the Qur'an of Belfast,"[79] but millions of poor have opted for the real Qur'an. So, if we appeal to the poor of the world to find out what is really going on in society and politics, we will soon find ourselves living in a very different world from that depicted by any version of Marx we may care to favor. Once we let the poor speak for themselves and tell their own stories, we will quickly discover that they present radically different stories from the quasi-Marxist stories presented on their behalf by their self-appointed representatives in liberation theology.

The Illusions of Pacifism

Would it help if we turned to pacifism? The central idea of pacifism is that disputes are to be settled without recourse to violence or force. One obvious advantage of pacifism is that it provides immediate moral justification for the rejection of terrorism. If recourse to violence is generally rejected, then terrorism is rejected; other ways of resolving disputes must be sought. The problem is that the cure proposed by pacifism turns out to be worse than the disease. By rejecting all use of lethal force, we are bereft of crucial resources in protecting innocent people from deadly attack. Applied to the response to terrorism, pacifism would require that we respond to terrorism without the use or sanction of lethal force. We would have to deal with terrorism without armed police and without soldiers. More generally pacifism entails that we have to construct states without recourse to the ultimate sanction of force. On the face of it, this whole way of thinking is nonsensical. It is not surprising that few can take this option seriously, once they attend to its implications. It requires a very special kind of intellectual malfunction and self-deception to sustain pacifism over time.

Yet the commitment to pacifism dies hard. It is useful to sort out the crucial options by means of distinction. On the one hand, there are pragmatic pacifists who hold that rejecting the use of lethal force will actually work in the end, even in disputes with terrorism. The claim in this instance is empirical: if we seek out and catalogue non-lethal ways to resolve disputes, these tested practices will work

[79] Ibid., 122.

as a response to terrorism. On the other hand, there are religious pacifists who ground their rejection of lethal force in divine revelation. The claim in this instance is theological: God requires us to eschew the use of lethal force to resolve disputes whatever the costs in suffering and death. One can, of course, mix and match the grounding here, but it is important to be clear exactly what is on offer and not to equivocate on the relevant evidence.

Pragmatic pacifists have tried hard in recent years to develop the practices that would implement their vision of dispute resolution. This important enhancement of the pacifist tradition flies under the banner of just peacemaking. It looks to evidence from political science and the history of the prevention of war; it thus aims to be persuasive across the board to all people of good sense and good will. Thus far ten practices have been identified as critical to just peacemaking: (1) nonviolent direct action; (2) independent initiatives to reduce threat; (3) cooperative conflict resolution; (4) acknowledging responsibility for conflict and injustice and seeking repentance and forgiveness; (5) advancing democracy, human rights, and religious liberty; (6) fostering just and sustainable economic development; (7) working with emerging cooperative forces in the international system; (8) strengthening the United Nations and international efforts for cooperation and human rights; (9) reducing offensive weapons and weapons trade; and (10) encouraging grass-roots peacemaking groups and voluntary associations.[80]

While there is an air of repetitive realism in and around this new version of pacifism, it totally fails as an adequate response to terrorism for a host of reasons. If we extract the appeal to divine revelation and take it on its merits as an empirical proposal, it works off a series of generalizations that can be twisted and turned to fit any situation to bring about the desired results. If we keep enough balls in the air as the causes of terrorism, should we deploy this or that just peacemaking practice, we can always conveniently select whatever balls we need in order to fool ourselves that peace would have occurred or that peace will occur. The explanations and predictions offered are always sufficiently vague or open-textured to allow for expedient revision. The carefully constructed air of science is bogus

---

[80]This list of practices was developed by a network of scholars and can be found in Glen Stassen, ed., *Just Peacemaking: Ten Practices for Abolishing War* (Cleveland: Pilgrim Press, 1998).

and misleading. With terrorism we are dealing first and foremost with human agents and their actions; we are not simply dealing with physical events and their causes. So this whole way of identifying the problems and working on proposed solutions is a recipe for intellectual and practical illusion.

Glen Stassen, for example, argues that "democratic states with human rights almost never directly make war against other democratic states with human rights…"[81] Clearly this provides no help in making sense of Irish terrorism, or in resolving it. Nor does it illuminate terrorism in the democratic states of India, Pakistan, and Indonesia. Moreover, the claim is immediately subject to massive qualifications. Stassen continues: "…although admittedly the U.S. funded and supported the overthrow of the popular government of Iran that brought the Shah to power, the overthrow of the Alliende government in Chile that brought the notorious Pinochet to power, and the contras in Nicaragua that sought to topple the democratically elected Sandinista government by means of terrorism, etc."[82] The grand causal claim about the beneficial effects of democracy has collapsed before it even gets off the runway.

Put differently, the revised project ignores the radical particularity of terrorist organizations and activity. Terrorism in Ireland was brought to its knees in part because inside agents trained by the state infiltrated the IRA to the highest levels and hopelessly compromised its operations. We can always propose that there could have been other ways to get the terrorists to stop killing innocent civilians for political purposes; but these just-so stories are always possible; they ignore the radically contingent activity of human agents. We can dress up these proposals in terms of a new paradigm, claim demonstrations on the basis of empirical research, talk incessantly about root causes, develop what seem to be law-like generalizations, but such rhetoric is self-deceiving. In the end what we get are a raft of moral and political recommendations dressed up as empirical research; we are presented with limiting platitudes masquerading as fact.

In time we may be able to harvest a host of insights from pragmatic pacifism that may be of value politically in resolving dis-

---

[81] Glen Stassen, "Turning Attention to Just Peacemaking Initiatives that Prevent Terrorism," in *Bulletin of the Council of Societies for the Study of Religion 31*, no. 3 (September 2002), 12.
[82] Ibid.

putes. However, these insights belong in the mix of factors that play within the political arena rather than as one element in some grandiose new paradigm for preventing terrorism. Otherwise, they are really partisan political judgments that are given an intellectually privileged position that cut off pertinent debate. At their best they represent a network of practices that anyone committed to peace will be glad to implement. Once they are set up as an alternative to appropriate military options, they are likely to kindle false hopes, if not actually foster further terrorist activity.

Religious pacifists are right to reject the logic of pragmatic pacifism. Their case does not rely on a happy outcome to just peacemaking practices; they simply see pacifism as a practice in and of itself. They oppose the use of lethal force as a matter of principle. In the Christian case they accept this principle as a matter of obedience to the divine will. While they readily commit to peacemaking practices, their commitment to pacifism in no way depends on their success. Indeed they may well reject the logic of pragmatic pacifism; they expect and accept suffering and death rather than engage in the lethal use of force.

Accepting suffering and death is not an irrational option in this instance, for the commitment to pacifism in this instance is grounded in divine revelation. Given that divine revelation is the strongest possible warrant for a course of action, religious pacifists refuse to allow suffering and death to count as a decisive counter-argument against their position. They may well feel the temptation to take up arms in self-defense or to protect their neighbors, but such temptation is to be resolutely resisted. In the most recent forms of Christian pacifism proponents have stressed that the practice of pacifism rests substantially on essential church practices without which the commitment to pacifism will fail. The practice of pacifism becomes a matter of faith from top to bottom. Both its grounding and its execution depend on divine revelation and divine grace as mediated through Jesus in the church. The issue is theological: Jesus Christ, fully human and fully divine, revealed how we should live (he rejected the use of lethal power); manifested the consequences of such living (suffering and death); committed his followers to forgiveness and reconciliation (in his life and moral mandates); and made available the power to live in this manner (in his resurrection and through Pentecost). Once we step inside this world, we need no further warrant for pacifism. Nor can we give reasons for stepping inside the world of divine revelation, for the commitment to divine revelation is ultimate; it does not rest on reason.

Stanley Hauerwas goes even further and insists that the truth about politics and war can only be known inside his world of divine revelation.

> Christians believe that the true history of the world, that history that determines our destiny, is not carried by the nation-state. In spite of its powerful moral appeal, this history is the history of godlessness. Only the church has the stance, therefore, to describe war for what it is, for the world is too broken to know the reality of war. For what is war but the desire to be rid of God, to claim for ourselves the power to determine our meaning and destiny? Our desire to protect ourselves from our enemies, to eliminate our enemies in the name of protecting the common history we share with our friends, is but the manifestation of our hatred of God.[83]

Consequently those educated, say, at Goshen College (a college sponsored by the Mennonite Church, one of the pacifist Christian denominations) are in a better position to know the truth about the political world than those educated at Duke University. In a flattering Commencement Address at Goshen, Hauerwas makes the point simply and clearly.

> For political science is not taught at Goshen College the way it is taught at Duke, since political science at Goshen is not at the service of nation/state ideologies. The history you learn is different because you know you are members of a community more determinative than the power called the United States of America. You learned to distrust abstract claims about objectivity because you are part of the people of the Second Chance that learned long ago that such claims are used to silence the voices of dissent.[84]

Hauerwas' vision of the nation-state is now obsolete, as I will indicate later. More importantly, his reductionist and simplistic descriptions of war are so obviously false that they undercut his claim to possess an exclusively privileged access to the truth about war through the church. Hauerwas does not, moreover, provide a persuasive account of where to locate the true church that delivers such

---

[83]Stanley Hauerwas, "Should War be Eliminated," in John Berkham and Michael Cartwright, *The Hauerwas Reader* (Durham: Duke University Press, 2001), 420.
[84]"Why Truthfulness Requires Forgiveness," *The Hauerwas Reader*, 315.

coveted goods. Truth to tell, he has difficulty in coming to terms with the reality of the terrorism of the IRA. Thus he is perfectly happy to allow the IRA's self-description of its activity as war rather than terrorism. "War is relative to each people's history. We thus often seek to deny to the other side the right to describe their violence as war. For example, barbarians cannot be warriors since they do not fight in a civilized manner. A bombing in London by the IRA is terrorism, not war."[85] What this really means is that terrorists can make up their own self-serving descriptions of their evil actions and get a free ride from Hauerwas and his disciples. Hauerwas is clearly incapable in this instance of distinguishing between truth and propaganda. What his particular observations reveal is not that theologians of his school have privileged access to the truth but that their judgments are subject to intellectual corruption. At this level it is often not the pious insider but the perceptive outsider who can help us know what is at stake. To put this theologically, we might say that the truth is often more visible through common grace than through special grace; there are weeds as well as tares in the truth claims of any church.

The arrival of Islam as a serious player in the West shows how parochial and unpersuasive Hauerwas' influential version of Christian pacifism has become. Radical Islamists and Christian pacifists can agree that revelation should be taken as a decisive warrant for action. If we cannot see the crucial status they ascribe to divine revelation, then we have not understood the concept of divine revelation and how it naturally and rightly functions. An acute problem is immediately generated when we are confronted, as we now are, with rival visions of the identification and meaning of divine revelation. Radical Islamists appeal to a divine revelation that gives them warrant for engaging in terrorism; Christian pacifists appeal to a divine revelation that gives them warrant for rejecting the use of lethal force. If both sides can rest pat on divine revelation, then both can claim legitimacy. If both insist that reason can only operate inside their chosen worlds of divine revelation, then we simply have to take it or leave it. We have to take their word for it that they got it right on divine revelation. But taking their word for it leaves us now with competing revelations in which one gives warrant for war and the other gives warrant for pacifism. We are in a hopeless

---

[85] *The Hauerwas Reader*, 420, fn. 43.

impasse.

Christian pacifists have the additional problem of securing the claim that divine revelation in the Christian tradition provides warrant for pacifism. As in the case of radical Islamists who claim sanction for terrorism, their claim is a minority report. The standard and correct objection at this point is that Christian pacifists have taken isolated elements in the teaching of Jesus, say, in the Beatitudes, that are meant to apply between persons, and extended them to apply between state and state, or between states and their citizens. They fail to see that the anger of God in judgment is the anger of love without hate. They sin the sin of refusing the God-given vocation to exercise the office of arrest and judgment. They cannot see that love in public relations "takes the form of mutual respect, of law, justice, liberty, and even help—especially to the weak."[86] As a consequence of these mistakes Christian pacifists are bereft of positive illumination when it comes to the right ordering of our political life together. In reality they either opt out of political life altogether, or they fall back upon the platitudes of pragmatic pacifism, or they buy into negative stereotypes of the state and nation that correlate conveniently with their theological commitments.

In the latter case they accept unwary generalizations about consumerism, globalization, capitalism, and the nation state. These judgments deploy lots of moral energy, but they do not begin to capture the actual realities we currently face. Christian pacifists are certainly very clear on what not to do in response to terrorism; we are not permitted to use lethal force under any circumstances. This is simple and straightforward. However, we are given no real help in moving forward positively. There are few, if any, robustly pacifist networks of political policy available as live options. The pacifist option might mean, for example, the immediate disbandment of the Defense Department and the reallocation of its funds, say, to overseas aid or to tax-relief. It might mean the replacement of armed police with unarmed security officers. Options like these are rarely canvassed, of course, because they represent political lalaland. In the meantime, then, pacifists are freeloaders within the current social and political arrangements.

---

[86] P. T. Forsyth, *The Christian Ethic of War* (London: Longmans, Green, and Co., 1916), 192.

Two Cheers for Just War Theory

We are, at least initially, given help on relevant political choices when we turn to the option of just war theory. The central motivation driving just war theory as we have received it from Augustine, Ambrose, and Aquinas is this: love of our neighbors requires that we protect them when they are assaulted by violent evil. Love is not just a matter of refraining from violence but of doing all we can to help our neighbors. It is one thing to refuse to engage in violence when we ourselves are attacked; it is another to refuse to use violence to protect other people who are unjustly attacked. Standing aside and letting others kill innocent civilians is refusing to take responsibility for helping other people. So we should be prepared to do all we can, up to and including using lethal force to stop terrorists from killing innocent people.

Again it is useful to sort out the crucial issues at stake by means of a distinction. On the one hand, there is a maximalist version of the just war tradition. In this case proponents work from a network of tough criteria, which, if satisfied, would underwrite the morally positive justification of the use of lethal force. On the other hand, there is a minimalist version of the just war tradition. In this case, proponents reject the drive for a network of tough criteria, preferring instead to rely on informed judgment, and they reject the whole notion of a positive moral justification for the lethal use of force in all circumstances.

A hallmark of the maximalist version is the drive to codify the criteria governing the use of lethal force. The crucial elements involved in just war as applied to terrorism can be easily catalogued. (1) The war on terror must repair or prevent some grave wrong, e.g. restore rights wrongly done away with, or reestablish a more just political order. (2) The war on terror must be declared by the legitimate authority, say, by president, congress, or parliament. (3) Government must declare the aims of the war on terror, e.g. destroy al-Qaeda, remove the Taliban, and work for a better Afghanistan. (4) The war on terror must be engaged in as a last resort, e.g. after negotiation fails, or if negotiation simply will not work. (5) In a just war on terror there must be a reasonable chance of success. (6) There must be proportionality, that is, we should not resort to a war on terror if the consequences would likely be worse than not doing so. Strenuous efforts to prevent negative, likely consequences need to be made. (7) There must be a right intention. Hatred and revenge are not appropriate; there must be a real intention to get rid of terrorism and to restore genuine peace. (8) Just means must be used in carrying out the war on terror. Hence we must distinguish between combatants and non-combatants, aim at military targets, and keep destruction proportionate to the achievable just ends in view.

While I admire the idealism at work in the maximalist position, it fails by setting in place dubious operational and moral straight-jackets that may aid good judgment if used flexibly but undercut it if deployed as an absolute code. The language of the war on terror may be central to masking one of the crucial problems we face at this point. Just as there was merit in speaking of a Cold War in the twentieth century, there is merit in speaking metaphorically of a War on Terror in the twenty-first. The metaphor of a war on terror draws attention to the fact that we are not dealing with mere politics, that we are facing the use of lethal force, that crucial national interests are at stake, and that conventional civilian defenses (like responding to terrorists as mere criminals) are inadequate to deal with the enemy. However, there cannot literally be a war on terror, for terror is simply one tactic in a network of tactics deployed to gain political ends. Thus a critical assumption that we need to have in place in order to apply a strong version of just war theory is missing. There is no conventional enemy, complete with a state and a conventional army; and there is often no standard declaration of war. In addition, it is often impossible to determine a reasonable chance of success and to work out a just sense of proportionality by way of response.

We can, of course, insist that it is enough if we can apply most of the criteria of just war theory, even if we have to apply them in a rather relaxed manner. This is in keeping with the historical development behind the whole just war debate. The list of criteria I cited is, in fact, the final stage of a process of codification that has gone on over centuries. The move to codify is a later development; it is an effort to formalize our best informal judgments. So we should not worry too much if there is slippage here or there in the application of old insights to a new situation. The overall aim is to set limits to the use of lethal force and thus to come away in the end with a good conscience, that is, with a sense that we have engaged in a just rather than unjust war. We want to be able to say with a straight face that we have been morally just in our use of lethal force.

By now the maximalist position is clearly coming under severe strain. We have accepted that one crucial condition for the very application of just war theory is missing (there is no war); we have conceded that crucial conditions of application have been abandoned (chances of success and proportionality); and we have reinterpreted the history of the tradition of just war as the development of diverse critical insights (rather than a code of conduct). All that is left is the claim that we are still acting justly. In reality we are knocking on the door of the minimalist version of just war theory. I think that dealing appropriately with terrorism requires us to walk through that door without apology.

What is critically at stake in responding to terrorism is that we be justified in what we do rather than that we be just in what we do; it would be wonderful to be just, of course, but justice is not always possible. It is this insight (that we be justified in what we do) that lies at the base of the just war tradition. The aim is both to set limits to the use of lethal force and to foster a robust debate across the board in political, legal, and military circles about where those limits are. Put differently, the goal is not to give up on justice, but to recognize that there are circumstances when the ideal of justice is impossible; thus we have to work on what is the least of the evil options available to us and to argue our judgments about this openly in the public domain. The move to codify best practices in this arena is a worthy one, but it is never final, and we should be wary of assigning positive moral worth to our actions even when we satisfy our best formal criteria. As P. T. Forsyth insisted: "It is not urged that war may be made in order to do good but to prevent the prevention of good, to resist wrong, and especially wrong to those who cannot resist for themselves."[87]

Underneath any codification there lies the ineradicable hand of human judgment without which we would never have any codification in the first place. This judgment may be wise or unwise, informed or uninformed, good or bad; it will always be imperfect, bound by the light of hindsight, and open to question by intelligent critics. It cannot be cast into some fully reliable method that will eradicate trust in fallible human agents and fallible human discernment, trained on particular challenges. There is no guarantee that

[87]Forsyth, *The Christian Ethic of War*, 87.

we will be just at this level of our lives. We can and should insist that we be justified by way of prudence, intelligence, and the best moral sense we can muster. We will be exceptionally fortunate if we have political, legal, and military leaders who can measure up to this logically imprecise but intellectually exacting standard.

It is important to understand what is at stake in this minimalist version of the just war tradition as applied here to terrorism. There is no claim that what we do represents an effort to establish the kingdom of God on earth. There is no hint of claiming divine sanction, or of any direct appeal to divine revelation. There is no effort to claim any kind of high moral ground. What is at stake is the goal of protecting the innocent, of restraining evil, and of doing so in a manner that may indeed be morally permissible but is likely to be shot through with tragedy, moral dissonance, and even a bad conscience. Yet there is equally no pulling back from using the best practices of dispute resolution; there is no abandoning of relevant (though contested and changing) rules of military engagement; there is no distribution of blank moral checks to be filled in at will; there is no setting up of the state action as criterion of moral action; there is no withdrawal into a private world of secrecy disconnected from public evaluation; and there is no reduction of moral and political reason to mere technical reason. In short, there is no move to cut military and political action loose from morality to let them swing free from ethical and theological evaluation. The underlying assumptions are these: the world is shot through with evil and sin; people deliberately and systematically reject the full resources of grace in their private and public lives; the default position in human life is war not peace (it is conflict not harmony); and the contingencies these assumptions entail must be taken radically seriously.

On the Edge of the Apocalypse

In dealing with terrorism we live on the edge of a moral apocalypse. In order to respond to it, some of those responsible for the welfare of others may land in places where our standard moral markers have been destroyed. In such circumstance the only moral compass they may remain is the mandate to do the least bad thing in the circumstances. The best move we can make by way of the justification of our actions is that we do the least evil we can, given all the options available. We can engage in justified action, but the depth of evil that we face has obliterated the option of just action or just war.

World War II can serve as a precedent. The challenge presented by the emergence of total war was unparalleled. There was no limit to what Adolf Hitler would do in eliminating Jews, in killing non-combatants of enemy nations, and in the enforced coercion of his own civilians in the war with the Allies. If he had succeeded, the outcome would have been utterly catastrophic on all fronts for victors and vanquished. In responding there is no question but that Winston Churchill led the Allies into reactions that failed the tests of the just war tradition as developed by the maximalist. The chances of success were precarious; there were very mixed intentions; the proportionality was highly questionable; and there were systematic, unrestrained attacks on non-combatants. Not surprisingly there was a heated moral and theological debate in England at the time, as represented by Bishop George Bell of Chichester and Bishop Cyril Garbett of York. Bell was convinced that the Allies were guilty of barbarism; Garbett argued that the choice was between the lesser of two evils. The dispute was never resolved; honest differences still remain; both were right.

It is no surprise that the kind of destruction and suffering involved in World War II can lead us to reach for language that goes beyond mere secular description for words borrowed from the language of faith. Observers of and participants in the terror let loose on civilians during that war, found themselves in exactly these circumstances.[88] They naturally spoke of living through the apocalypse, of doomsday scenarios, of facing hell on earth, of enduring experiences that were worse than the end of the world. Prosaic descriptions of evil as, say, unspeakably wicked or heinous, did not do justice to what was faced. Were terrorists to go nuclear, we would be in the same position. As in the case of some forms of conventional warfare, we are already in this position with current forms of terrorist activity. After being lulled into a sense of false security with the end of the Cold war, we are now back living in an apocalyptic world. The nuclear option is back on the table; and we have even fewer moral constraints in place in the social and political arena than we had in the early part of the twentieth century. No doubt some would like us to hand it all over to lawyers, but there is no reason to think that a band of lawyers will be any wiser than a

---

[88] Jörg Friedrich's *The Fire: The Bombing of Germany 1940–1945* (New York: Columbia University Press, 2006) makes this abundantly clear.

group of politicians. We will need to have all hands on deck in the debate to find our way forward.

No Stable States

We also inhabit a wider political and international context that is subject to ongoing, systematic change. We live neither in a time when the state had its own theological ideology that excluded Christian voices and action in the public square, nor in a time when Christian leaders occupy and control the organs of state. In the first scenario it was natural that much of the church was pacifist; in the second it was natural that a more maximalist version of just war theory worked relatively well. Many think we can legitimately see our current situation as more or less identical with these two options. The description of the wider context is crucial at this point. Some think we are in a nation state that has its own secular ideology and idols. Others say we are living in a new Empire run by Christian Fundamentalists, free market capitalists, neo-conservatives, or some combination of the same. So we live either in a confessionalist secular state or in a new version of Christendom.

Both these proposals are empirically mistaken. For one thing the new Empire has no stable theological clothes. It exists in the eye of its beholders as a mixture of theology, economic theory, and secular political philosophy that cannot be said to be a state-imposed theology in any serious sense of that term. We can say the same about the ideology of the nation-state. The nation state as we have had it in the United States simply does not have a secure theology; it has a fascinating civil religion, but that is another matter entirely. Politicians, whatever they may say, are pretty much forced to be functional atheists in the public arena.

However, there is something more deeply wrong in these analyses. Both options are simply obsolete; we live neither in a New Empire nor in a nation-state; these are false descriptions of the world we actually inhabit. The state in the West has itself changed dramatically in the last generation. It has moved from a nation state to become a market state.[89] Nation states can control their boundaries, their economies, their cultures, and their security; they seek to provide in varying degrees health care, education, and old-age security. A cocktail of changes in communications, technology, the

[89] Philip Bobbitt's *The Shield of Achilles: War, Peace, and the Course of History* (New York: Alfred A. Knopf, 2002) provides a fine account of this development.

failure of socialism, and globalization have undermined the nation state. In their place we have market states. Market states concentrate on maximizing opportunity. They balance public and private means of delivering public goods; and they look to the market place and its practices as a criterion of success in what they do. This is true of Moscow, London, Tokyo, Brussels, Berlin, Dublin, Seoul, and the like. Politics and religion reflect the background music of the market state. So we have market churches, market preachers, and market research driven politicians. Even philanthropy is now administered on the model of market practices. We can rave and rant all we want about this, but this is where we now live. It will take time for the new religious, political, legal, and military dust to settle; it is not surprising that we feel blinded and disoriented.

In the meantime, when the terrorists come knocking down my door, I want to have soldiers and a helicopter nearby. I also want a robust church in the neighborhood that has a saint or two in its midst and that is able to form effective politicians to work in the public domain.

7

The Paddy Factor

The Church in Politics

One way to identify the role of the church in responding to terrorism is to determine the Paddy factor in society and politics.

By the church I simply mean the Christian bodies and denominations we know in the West. By politics I mean the general form of representative democracy with which we are familiar in western society. By the Paddy factor I mean the peculiar contribution the church, given its nature and mission, may make to society and politics as these relate to terrorism.

Politics is absolutely crucial here because the practice of terrorism is intimately related to politics; after all terrorism is the deployment of terror to achieve political goals. Hence in determining the Paddy factor we need to focus not just on terrorism but also on that wider world without which terrorism would not even exist. Here, of course, we meet a massive roadblock, for many want to eliminate the Paddy factor from politics. They think that dragging religion into politics is a disaster; religion is part of the problem not of the solution. There is widespread paranoia that the Paddy factor will foster terrorism rather than inhibit it. I shall in due course tackle this more general challenge head on; banning the Paddy factor from the public square, I shall argue, is anti-democratic, illiberal, and futile.

In inventing this new name (the "Paddy factor") for capturing dimensions of the life of faith in society and politics I am, of course, transposing a name to a noun. The originating figure that makes Paddy such an endearing designation is the great St. Patrick, patron saint of Ireland throughout the year and patron saint of the whole world on March 17. When I was growing up in and around Enniskillen, St. Patrick was not part of our memory bank. Patrick belonged to the other side, to the enemy, an icon that was used by Roman Catholics against Protestants in the war of truth in religion. We did not celebrate St. Patrick's Day; and we had only the faintest notion of who he was and what he accomplished. This attitude can still be found in Belfast. In the run-up to St. Patrick's Day in 2007 a schoolboy in Sandy Row in Belfast still thought that St. Patrick was a pope. As good Protestants we were not much interested in saints; they had become a snare in the history of the church that needed purging. Moreover, I had no idea that the area around Enniskillen was once a monastic center that was famous for its biblical scholarship in the Dark Ages, when the Celtic Church sent out its missionaries to evangelize Europe. There is even a hint of the importance of biblical scholarship in the legend that the prophet Jeremiah was buried on the monastic site at Devenish Island on Lough Erne just outside Enniskillen.

St. Patrick as a Model

Patrick was not a politician; he was a saint, an evangelist, and a bishop of the church. It is profitable to linger on his life and work as we proceed. We are fortunate to have two of his own letters to consult in sorting out his significance. They make clear that his first commitment was to the church, to its treasures, its practices, and above all to the power and love of God that he discovered for himself. This prioritizing is critical in any sane account of the relation between the church and politics.

Brought up within a Christian family in Britain, his spiritual life caught fire when he was captured, carried off to Ireland, and put to work as a slave in Co. Mayo. Given his suffering and isolation he learned how to pray. He also learned to trust God, to lean on the voice and providence of God. So much so, that when he had a vision of a boat that was awaiting him he took off on an arduous journey to the sea. He found the boat. He was at first repelled and then welcomed on board by its pagan captain. Reaching land after three days, they took off on foot, and everything went well until they lost their way. After twenty-eight days they ran out of food.

The captain admonished Patrick:

> "How now Christian? You say your God is great and all-powerful; why then can't you pray for us? For we are in danger of starving; it will go hard with us ever to see a human being again." I said confidently to them: "Turn sincerely with all your heart to the Lord my God, because nothing is impossible to Him, so that today He may send you food in your way until you are satisfied, because he has abundance everywhere."[90]

Food appeared soon afterwards in the form of a herd of pigs. It was small wonder that Patrick became instantly honorable among his pagan companions. In due course he found his way home to his family.

Called in a series of visions to return to Ireland as a missionary, he underwent a deep mystical experience of the Holy Spirit that enabled him to withstand intense opposition from his seniors in the church. His experience of the love and power of God shine through his letters. The details of his labors in Ireland in the fifth century remain unknown, but the general outcome is now justly famous. He worked sensitively with the local leaders, baptized thousands, set up an effective church structure, and conducted his ministry with unceasing integrity. In time he established a vibrant Christian community that transformed the pagan culture of his day without destroying its best treasures. He laid the foundations for the creation of the monastic tradition that combined scholarship, agricultural labor, and missionary enterprise. We are not playing host to the romantic overkill of the recent past if we say that the life of St. Patrick was a conspicuous success. He helped provide the initial resources for making available the Celtic tradition in written and not just verbal form, for preserving the very best of Greco-Roman culture, and for keeping alive the deep faith of the church in a period of savagery and darkness.

One of the forgotten elements in the life of St. Patrick was the tough line he took towards those who killed innocent civilians. The soldiers of Coroticus, a chieftain-king from Scotland, rightly earned his wrath when they raided Ireland and brutally took a large contingent of his converts captive. They killed some of them and sold others into slavery. In a letter now lost St. Patrick tried privately to gain their release. Coroticus dismissed that letter with contempt

---

[90] Daniel Conneely, *St. Patrick's Letters: A Study of Their Theological Dimension* (Maynooth: An Sagart, 1993), edited by Patrick Bastable et al, 66–7.

and mockery. St. Patrick then wrote publicly, not mincing his words on the final fate of Coroticus and his soldiers. He predicted they would be banished to become slaves of hell in everlasting punishment. He also banished them from the church. "Consequently let every God-fearing person know that they are excommunicate from me and from Christ my God for whom I am an ambassador. Parricides! Fratricides! Ravenous wolves gobbling up the people of the Lord like bread on the table."[91] Even then he showed remarkable magnanimity should there be repentance and a change of heart. He finishes his letter on a conciliatory note.

> But if God inspires them to return, at some time or another, to a right mind towards God, so that even at a late hour they repent of such an impious deed—murder of the brethren of the Lord—and so release the baptized women captives they previously seized: if God thus inspires them, so that they deserve to live unto God and be made whole here and in eternity, peace be to them with the Father and the Son and the Holy Spirit.[92]

The Limitations and Promise of Church Action

With the life of St. Patrick as our background music we can now turn to the central question before us. How should we spell out the Paddy factor and its place in society and politics? What is the role of the church in this arena? And within that role how might it do its best work in responding to the challenge of terrorism?

We begin with a sober observation. Terrorists, like the ravenous wolves of Coroticus they are, direct their violence first and foremost against innocent people. Of course, they also do all they can to destroy symbolic buildings and the economic infrastructure, but to achieve maximum impact they kill civilians. The state and its agents are therefore of necessity the first to come to the aid of its suffering citizens. The church is not the first line of defense; it is the state that has this coveted role. There is no way that churches can or should take on the multifaceted response to terrorism represented by politicians, the police, the medical professions, the army, and the like. Churches are not formally in the business, say, of training and supplying military intelligence, a critical factor in dealing with terrorism. We see here an intrinsic limit on what can be done to respond to terrorism on the part of the church. Other limits are set

[91] Ibid., 77.
[92] Ibid., 81.

by the political arrangements within which churches operate. Thus in a representative democracy, the distinction, if not the separation, of church and state does not allow, for example, that a bishop be the president or the head of state. Still other limits arise from the side of the church. Thus most churches will support the presence of chaplains in the armed forces but they will not give funding directly to a war effort. In fact the primary role that churches can now formally play in relation to terrorism is indirect. It has an impact insofar as it influences politics and the life of its host culture generally. The Paddy factor is a modest factor; it cannot and should not take on the heavy lifting in response to terrorism.

These radical limitations of the role of the church in society are a recent development. There have been times from the days of Constantine down to the nineteenth century when churches and its leaders were the leading agents of society and culture. Bishops and popes have been princes, diplomats, and soldiers. Clearly those days are now gone forever; few, if any, want to return to them.

Yet it is important not to exaggerate. Even on a formal level churches can have a pivotal role in society in relation to terrorism at a cultural and moral level. They can create task forces to address specific issues; they can have permanent agencies that work on thorny political questions; and they can make relevant pronouncements in their assemblies. It is easy to be cynical about the impact of this kind of work; much of it can be partisan and ephemeral; much of it sits on shelves and on websites unread. A lot of it is incompetent, showing inadequate factual, moral, and intellectual grasp of the complex issues that need to be addressed.[93] However, this kind of work has an important place in providing information, in raising important questions, and in creating a climate where deliberation is taken seriously, a pivotal factor in any healthy democracy.

There is also space for the prophetic voice that arises above partisan politics and calls a whole community to come to its senses. Self-appointed prophets are, to be sure, easily acquired because easily appointed; but when the real thing shows up, they are a great gift. They articulate a moral clarity about issues that is apt and enduring. Moreover, there are moments when respected church leaders

---

[93] This is clearly the case with "Countering Terrorism: Power, Violence and Democracy Post 9/11, a Report by a Working Group of the Church of England's House of Bishops," published in September 2005 and available to download at www. churchofengland.org/media/45505/terrorism.pdf [accessed January 7, 2013].

can step into the political arena and, for shorter or longer periods, provide temporary political leadership. Or they can do things that cannot be done by those who are part of the conventional political process. They can represent crucial interests or break dysfunctional processes precisely because they stand outside the contested power blocks of interest in society and politics. If they outstay their welcome, they tend to become a pretentious nuisance, reduced to becoming talking heads that are ineffective and mostly do more harm than good. There are few sights more pathetic than church leaders putting their political underwear on display in public.

What is at issue here is a crucial division of labor within the life of the church. The regular work of pastors, preachers, priests, deacons, and bishops should be directed to the welfare of the church and its ministries. This is the work for which they have been trained and for which they are ordained. They misread their vocation when they set themselves up as political activists and proxy-agents of the state. When they engage in pavement politics they are often the dupes of their own self-importance. If clergy really want to become serious political players, they should resign their positions, abandon their secure salaries and pension plans, and stand as candidates in relevant elections. In this way they can take responsibility for their views in the rough and tumble of political debate rather than rely on some phony mystical privilege or use their office as a defense mechanism. We can also get rid of them when their ignorance and incompetence become publicly manifest and they become a menace to the public good.

What I opposing here is the sin of clericalism. Clericalism identifies the church with its pastoral leadership. The clear assumption is that the church is only at work in politics if clergy are publicly active. Clericalism dies hard in church circles; yet clericalism is a snare and a delusion. The really significant work of the church in politics lies in the hands of Christians who are deeply involved in the political process all the way from voting to holding the highest offices of government.

Yet more is at stake than a division of labor. The first task of the church is to be itself, that is, a body that is one, holy, catholic, and apostolic. As such it bears witness to a world that transcends and relativizes the whole political enterprise. One of the reasons that folk turned to terrorism in Ireland was because they had put the nation above everything else. They were prepared to kill and be killed in its name. Hence while the IRA, for example, readily used the symbols and practices of the Catholic Church to advance their cause, they were also fully prepared to set aside its moral and theological teaching. The primary allegiance to their brand of Irish nationalism trumped their baptism and the faith they professed. They co-opted the sentiments, concepts, and practices of the Christian faith to carry their nationalist ideology.

It was one of the besetting weaknesses of the Catholic Church in Ireland that it was deeply ambivalent in its own stance at this point. While church leaders readily condemned terrorism, they failed to deal with the underlying idolatry. They did not call into question crass exploitation of theological themes until it was a case of too little too late. They also, all too readily, provided soil within which terrorism could take root and flourish. While they did not provide propaganda for the cause, they happily supplied plenty of pre-propaganda. They accepted uncritically the glorification of heroes filled with hate, and they transmitted the historical myths that excused a cult of violence. One historian of the IRA perceptively identified the place of pre-propaganda in the cultivation of the soil in which terrorism could grow and flourish.

> Northern nationalists, educated in their own schools, joining only republican sporting and social clubs and influenced by a church that reflected their own fears and aspirations, had from early youth received 'pre-propaganda', the myths of ancient battles, of 1916 and the efficacy of violence. It was towards this target audience that the IRA applied its mobilisation propaganda.[94]

The relevance of these observations for mainstream Islam is obvious. If mainstream Muslims do not act aggressively, persistently, and systematically to confront radical Islam, they will simply become the agents of pre-propaganda and provide the soil where radical Islam latter will flourish and be sustained.

Christian Identity Trumps Political Idolatry

We are now at the stage where St. Patrick can help. Not only did he excommunicate the soldiers of Coroticus, he established the life of

---

[94]Maurice Tugwell, "Politics and Propaganda of the Provisional IRA," in Paul Wilkinson, *British Perspectives on Terrorism* (London: George Allen and Unwin, 1981), 20. Tugwell's judgment has been cogently confirmed by Rogelio Alonso in *The IRA and the Armed Struggle* (London: Routledge: 2003).

the Celtic Church with an identity that transcended local identities and politics. He thereby cut off the option of the idolatry of the nation at its roots. He created a church strong enough to challenge and excommunicate the murderers of his day.

St. Patrick's life was marked by a joyous inwardness that had a deep assurance of the power of God to change lives and to act providentially in the world. A radical freedom breathes through his writings, but it was not a freedom to be free from God but a freedom to serve God in the midst of poverty and violence. Nor was it a freedom that freed him from the life and ministry of the church, but a freedom that took him beyond his own resources, a freedom to rely on the canonical materials and practices of the church. We might say that St. Patrick drank deeply of the wine of a church whose bottles, however badly mishandled by the seniors who faulted him and put him on trial, were still full of the faith of the gospel. He worked from the assumption that the first great social work of the gospel was to create a new community that had its own canonical resources. The church also had its own internal doctrine, ethos, rigors, and discipline. It was not a cave of all the theological winds but a community rooted and grounded in divine revelation wrapped in scripture, creed, and other vital means of grace. It was possessed of a divine Word made available by the Spirit and articulated in a host of ways. It had resources that enabled it to withstand the lure of pagan and ethnic identity.

When I was trained in the 1960s and 70s, the working assumption of much academic theology was that the world would follow Europe in its loss of faith. In the intellectual wilderness that ensued, theologians scrambled to fix the faith so as to render it credible to its critics. In this process precious cargo was thrown overboard with enthusiasm; those who protested were dismissed as intellectually crippled and myopic. The kind of robust, industrial strength Christianity represented by St. Patrick was seen as hopelessly outdated. We now know that Christianity is flourishing in the Global South and that the obituary notices have turned out to be false. St. Patrick would, I suspect, be fully at home in the kind of faith that is now spreading outside the West. He would readily resonate with acts of deliverance from the demonic, with the readiness to expect God to work in miraculous power, with the love of scripture, and with the unembarrassed emphasis on the presence of the Holy Spirit. To be sure, these phenomena set our intellectual teeth on edge; they scare the life out of most conventional western Christians; they make some theologians vomit. So we will have to go back to school theologically and begin all over again in order to readjust. If this reformation gives us a headache, it also brings us back to something the church has always known. At its best, the church bears witness to a World that stands above our political realities; and that World calls us to a judgment that puts all our temporal interests in their proper place in the life of eternity.

It would be silly to fall into a romantic trance at this point. We cannot turn the clock back to the ancient Christianity of Ireland (where monasteries became its genetic backbone); nor can we simply import the faith of the Global South (where new institutional forms are still very much in the making and theological chaos abounds). We need to be open to all the resources that the Holy Spirit showers upon the church (ancient and modern), so that the church can be fully itself in our own time and space. This will not in itself bring terrorism to an end. Where grace abounds, sinners will still resort to violence against the innocent to achieve their political ends. However, the full working of the Holy Spirit will foster a church where terrorism will be morally outlawed and where the power of God can provide healing for those tempted to turn to it to reach their political goals. It will also be a church where its clerical leadership will discover their true vocation and stop lusting after temporal power and glory. We need a church that will be drawn into the fire of God's power and love and consumed by its purifying flames.

If the first calling of the church in a world of terrorism is to be itself and act as a brake on the inflated pretensions of politics and politicians, its second is to recover its intellectual nerve. This should begin with the relearning of the art of evangelism that goes way beyond the settling for cradle Catholicism or the hangovers of revivalism. We must implement a vision of Christian initiation that will foster the creation of genuine disciples; and we must develop ministries of evangelism that will be robust enough to convert terrorists. I propose that the threshold tests for new church members in the future be these. Can they testify with flair to their faith to their Islamic neighbors? Are they prepared to die for the faith? Can they begin to deal with the intellectual opposition to the faith in the

West? Can they intelligently and fruitfully engage in politics?

One of the most striking features of the evangelization of the Greco-Roman world and its climax in the conversion of the Irish was that many of its great teachers and theologians were evangelists.[95] Patrick was not a great theologian, but he worked from a rich version of the faith that was able to make a difference in the way his converts saw the world. The theology of the church of his time was intimately related to spiritual and intellectual formation. Thus the great themes of Christian theology from creation to the end of the world were derived from the impressive catechetical schools where the faith was handed over to new converts with creativity and flair. Teachers and evangelists believed that the gospel was given not just for the healing of the nations but also for the healing of individual souls. They knew that these were intimately related. They knew in their bones that church members must be sufficiently well formed in the faith to love their neighbors in the social and political arenas. Hence baptism involved immersion in the great sea of faith, not in shallow pools cut off from their originating source. Healthy forms of evangelism that take seriously initiation into the Kingdom of God and into the church are imperative for intelligent engagement with the culture and with politics.[96]

Such initiation is especially important for Christians who enter politics as their God-given vocation. The challenge here is simple. We cannot expect Christian politicians to survive, much less flourish, if they are not formed and equipped in a way that fits them to operate in the contentious world we now inhabit. They will need, of course, to be politically formed, so that they can actually work within the harsh political realities of elections, the media, bureaucracy, parties, caucuses, and the like. They must be skilled and effective politicians. Yet first and foremost they will need formation in the rich faith of the church. This in turn requires that the church be a deep church, so that it knows its own great treasures, that it lives from the power of the Holy Spirit, and that it can really form its members in an effective manner. It will be disastrous if leaders of state are brought to faith in a ship where the engines have been switched off and the crew has taken to using oars borrowed from

[95]Thus Origen, a theologian's theologian, spent years patiently winning Gregory the Wonderworker to the faith.

[96]My own vision of what this involves is laid out in *The Logic of Evangelism* (Grand Rapids: Eerdmans, 1989).

neighboring canoes to steer the vessel. It will be equally disastrous if the only food they serve in the kitchen is that borrowed from thin, faddish versions of the Christian faith.

As I noted earlier, the first line of defense in the war on terror is not the church but the state. The church rightly stands at a distance from the state, introducing the world to another World that stands in judgment on the state, providing another community rooted and grounded in the gospel. In fact terrorism brings the church face to face with its own identity, healing it of the superficiality and sentimentality that bedevils it in liberal societies. Terrorism breaks the bondage to thin forms of Christianity; by its brutality terrorism drives Christians back to older and deeper resources mediated through the language of sin and redemption. It forces its pastors and priests to find their proper identity and vocation as servants of the gospel and keepers of the faith of the Ages. Once this renewal of the church takes root, they can step back from their political pretensions and set laity free to enter into the life of the society and state, most especially as professional politicians. Once we abandon the sin of clericalism and recognize a proper division of labor between church and state, and between clerics and laity, then we can see the crucial role the church can play in society and politics through those lay members who become radically involved in the political enterprise. The primary agents of the church in politics are neither prophets, clerics, church councils, nor church agencies, but ordinary lay people who vote and who become politicians.

There is no need at this point to go into the details of what should be done by politicians in response to terrorism. To be sure, we can draw attention to the general principles that should readily be operative. The state should respect human rights, serve the common good, uphold justice, use lethal force only in justified circumstances, avoid partisan self-interest, and so on. We can expect heated debate about what principles should be adopted and how they should be applied. Christians will also legitimately disagree on the broader political philosophies that best serve the common good, whether they be conservative, liberal, or socialist. The church can help its members come to terms with the options by fostering the cultivation of political education in its schools and universities, but it would be wrong to make any political philosophy canonically binding. Divine revelation provides no blueprint for the ordering of political life; the church's members have honorably embraced a host of political insights, philosophies, practices, and policies. In this respect Christianity is radically different from both radical and mainstream forms of Islam.

In the end Christian politicians will have to take their life in their hands and work through the logistical details of what is required to contain and eliminate terrorism. In this they will, of course, draw on the skill of a host of experts, most especially the skills and experts of its military officers and all that lies back of their skills.[97] It is the privilege and responsibility of politicians to look after the lives of innocent civilians when terrorists show up. To offer any kind of logistical advice beyond that of any ordinary, informed citizen would be silly at this point. On these matters I am neither an expert nor the son of an expert.

There are, however, two more general issues that deserve attention. The first relates to the increasing opposition to believers in politics and the second concerns any Christian commitment to representative democracy. In both cases I want to clear the decks so that Christians will cease to be inhibited by the half-truths and nonsense that abound.

Resisting Secularist Intolerance

We all know that the move to secularization over the last two centuries means for many in modern representative democracies that the churches and their members are really a menace in politics. If churches exist, they and their flocks should stick to their own private world; they should return to the first days of the church before Constantine when they confined their work to spiritual matters; temporal matters belong to secularists or to religious believers who accept the constraints of secularism. Churches and their members should return to the grand old days of St. Patrick and stay there.

This is a bizarre proposal. First, the gospel and its articulation require not just the transformation of the individual and his or her private existence but also the transformation of all of creation,

---

[97] If we are committed to the use of lethal force in our response to terrorism, then the church dare not abandon those who have to do this work to fend for themselves. There are virtues and vices that come with the life of a soldier that need special care and attention. Happily this is now getting the attention it deserves. See, for example, Bernard J. Vernkamp, *The Moral Treatment of Returning Warriors in Early Medieval and Modern Times* (Scranton: University of Scranton Press, 2006).

including the human world of politics. Christians will love their neighbors politically; this is non-negotiable. So the move to restrict the faith in this manner cannot be squared with the demands of faith. Second, in a representative democracy it would be odd in the extreme to squelch the voices of serious believers, as if they do not have the rights and privileges of engaging in political life. This kind of selective democracy is a self-contradiction, an oxymoron; it is illiberal to the core. Third, to restrict real political engagement to self-confessed secularists or to religious believers who have been house trained to limit themselves to secular concepts and premises is to privilege one set of believers over against others. It is to establish a confessionalist secular state that in its own way imposes its secular ideologies on the rest of the population through legislation, education, and other organs and agencies of government.

It is very tempting for Christians to accommodate to secularist persuasion and propaganda at this point and enter into the public arena only on condition that they use secular reason to determine the outcome of political questions. We can see the merit in this proposal in that many of the issues that crop up in politics do indeed involve the use of empirical reason, that is, reliance on straightforward observation and scientific inquiry. In the light of this, it should not surprise us when many want to keep morality and religion at bay in politics. Our ruling elites have become public skeptics on morality; or, at least, they think they ought to be public skeptics. We are not, of course, public skeptics on matters of science and economics; we think that there is public truth in these domains than can be enacted in the public order. However, we are extremely nervous and wobbly about taking any kind of moral stance in government; we will hear moral claims only when politicians are sure they can get away with it; and then they are uttered like divine oracles. Morality (it is thought) is essentially a matter of private choice and opinion; hence the politicians should really remain morally neutral. If they go moral on us then they are likely to impose their moral agendas on the rest of us, and use the power of the state to camouflage their contested opinions. Given the close relation that exists between morality and religion, the distinction and separation between church and state reinforces our skittishness. We have a long memory of the folly of coercion in the arena of religion. Moreover, we are even more skeptical about religion than we are about morality. Hence it is difficult for believers to get a foothold in the public debate at any level; they may make profession of faith to gain votes, but they can operate as politicians only if they are functional atheists or agnostics.

The difficulties multiply when believers engage in political life in stupid and inappropriate ways. Believers sometimes fail to honor the distinction between the church and state. They demonize their opponents. They want miracles and magic in a world designed to be the fruit of human collaboration. They turn the divine into a holy labor-saving device that short-circuits the necessary engagement with bureaucratic processes. They introduce spooky causal agents that undermine human responsibility. They think that God sends his rain only on the righteous, and they act as if they are the darlings of heaven. They use pious discourse to win votes and raise funds. They indulge in churchy talk that spawns sentimentality and intellectual fog. They privilege the interests of their own faithful at the expense of the good of the whole. They turn to divine revelation when they should be consulting the practices of reason and good sense; they rely on theological cobwebs when technical inquiry is essential. They have grand principles but no realistic policies or strategies that can implement them; or they have policies that represent their party-political affiliation. They are impatient with imperfection and with sensible compromise. They grandly claim to speak for the poor when they live in mansions and have vast expense accounts. This catalogue of woe ignores, of course, the positive contributions that believers have made to politics; but when we are in the grip of a secularist theory, the exceptions prove the rule. And the rule is: robust believers are a menace in politics (except when they embrace the political fads of the day).

Political life, however, rests on far more than mere empirical observation and scientific inquiry. It is inescapably moral in orientation. States are not morally or intellectually neutral. This needs to be resolutely and steadfastly acknowledged. Once we see this, then the veto on Christians in political life is overturned.

To begin, Western democracies are not morally neutral on crucial matters related to the family, like marriage. Polygamy, polyandry, and bigamy are not permitted. For better or worse, the western democracies have adopted the remnants of a Christian conception of marriage, even though the justification for the practice may now no longer be Christian. The state is not morally neutral on marriage; to change the present conventions would not be an abdication of morality but a change in the moral choices of the state. Nor is the state morally neutral on such practices as racism, adoption, dueling, capital punishment, cruelty to animals, apartheid, bestiality, and incest.

Furthermore, the state, as understood in the current situation, is not neutral in its commitments on what it is to be human. In political life we cannot avoid taking sides on contentious issues in and around what human beings are. Consider the commitment to freedom of thought and action. The idea (beloved by confessional secularists) that persons should be allowed to exercise choice in metaphysical, moral, and religious matters is a claim about human agency. It gives expression to a particular vision of persons as independent individuals, on the liberty of the person as attainable through the absence of government constraints, and on the good of persons being instantiated in the political arrangements that make such independence and liberty possible. These are not neutral claims. They are themselves inescapably metaphysical and incurably contested; they involve a particular vision of human agency and destiny.

Furthermore, it is patently clear that the state will not always allow a wayward individual's metaphysical commitments to stand merely because the individual has chosen them. Consider the Marxist who rejects the current arrangements on property. He begins putting this vision into practice by leading the charge in taking over the means of production in his local neighborhood. He will not get to first base if he pleads his right to his personal choice of worldview as a defense when he is hauled into court for trespassing. The same can be said for anarchists who put their convictions in to practice. It is clear that where legislators and judges play the right-to-choose-your-own-vision-of-existence cards, this is not morally neutral at all; all sorts of possibilities have been screened out, while certain privileged and favored cases have been allowed to count as legitimate options on the meaning of human existence.

Nor is the state neutral in its commitments about the nature of knowledge. Nervousness about religion and morality is often tied to hidden assumptions about knowledge; it rests on the view that only science gives us truth. However, the nature and content of knowledge is as much contested as the nature and content of morality; the state and its agents are constantly called upon to make decisions on what we really know on any particular issue. To claim that science provides "public truth," and that morality and religion are a matter of "private truth," and then to rely on some such principle to keep moral and religious commitments out of the public arena, is to make a substantive commitment. This claim about public and private truth is not a scientific claim, nor is it a matter of public observation; it is what it has always been, that is, a substantive philosophical proposal to be discussed and debated like any other philosophical proposal.

If none of these arguments prove that politics is a moral enterprise, consider this final observation. The emergence of terrorism on an international scale has done to theories of state neutrality what the Scopes trial did to Fundamentalism in the 1920s. It has exposed them as a fraud. Terrorism has exposed our moral underwear once and for all. No serious government can sit on the sidelines and pretend that terrorism is a sober moral option in a representative democracy or in politics generally. Nor can it sit on its hands and not take action to protect its citizens. The crowbar of events has smashed overnight the conventional view of political reality as a neutral mechanism for resolving disputes between contesting parties.

We can capture our situation by saying that we live in a market state marked by radical pluralism. A ragbag of competing metaphysical, moral, theological, and atheological visions constitutes the modern cultural and political situation. This has resulted from a sweeping extension of freedom in politics over the last two hundred years. All over Europe in the nineteenth century, the political leaders of the old regimes of throne, aristocracy, and altar had to abandon their confessional states and throw open the doors of the political world to dissenters, Jews, Roman Catholics, agnostics, and atheists. The Paddies of the world had to be given their place in the political arena; or at least they had to be let in the back door.[98] We now know that Paddy is here to stay; and he should not take kindly to inappropriate house-training. He belongs in the market

[98] For a superb account of the situation in England before the demise of the confessional state see J. C. D. Clark, *English Society 1660–1832* (Cambridge: Cambridge University Press, 2000). For a competing analysis see Roy Porter, *The Making of the Modern World* (New York: W.W. Norton &Company, 2000).

state, and he is free to make his case to any who will listen and vote for him.

Paddy in fact should be warmly welcomed into the political arena. Representative democracies require the active engagement and participation of all their citizens. It may look as if the market state has turned politics into a whirlwind of advertising and manicured television debates, but the substantive practices of representative democracy are alive and well. We all can vote; we can find out where candidates stand; we can, if we take the trouble, cut through the hype and the pretension; we can get rid of corrupt and incompetent politicians after a season; and new political agents can try their hand at looking after the public good. Within this volatile process, Christian laity should take their place as active and professional politicians.

Defending Democracy

But should Christians be committed to representative democracy in the first place? We cannot quit the field without addressing this important question.

At one level this is a purely rhetorical question. Christians are committed to representative democracy because this is the world they meet when they get out of bed in the morning. St. Patrick took the world as he found it, and he then went to work with flair and ingenuity within it; so should contemporary Christians. Patrick's world was not, a democratic world. However, it is precisely the world of representative democracy that we now occupy; Christians should get on with the business of living in it to the glory of God and for the common good. Like it or not, God has now providentially placed us in a world of representative democracy. We have learned the hard way that moral and religious coercion are not the way of the gospel either religiously or politically. Christendom is gone; a Christian confessional state is no longer an option.[99] If Muslims and confessionalist secularists in the West want to change this, then Christians should challenge them theologically, intellectually, and politically. We have seen what these movies mean, and we have no intention of renting them; confessionalist states should be resisted by every means that are morally possible. We can and must draw a

[99] That this can still be a Christian option is suggested in a typically rich and subtle way by Charles Taylor in *A Catholic Modernity* (Oxford: Oxford University Press, 1999), 36–37.

distinction between church and state; once drawn we should pre-serve it. Given their own disastrous mistakes and coercive history, Christians, of all people, should insist on this hard-won political development.

However, rather than simply accept the status quo as we find it, Christians should develop their own vision of the foundations of democracy. We do not need to canonize representative democracy as a doctrine of the church, but we can explore why we committed to democracy because we are Christians. How we might articulate that commitment is an open question. Hence we can imagine a minimalist case in which it is argued that democracy is the worst form of government except any other. The primary theological warrant in this case would be an appeal to original sin: given their propensity to evil, folk are not to be trusted for too long with too much power, and democracy is a good mechanism to ensure this end. Alternatively, we might deploy a maximalist case in which it is argued that democracy is a fitting expression of the Christian faith in a pluralist world. Thus we might argue that everyone deserves respect and a vote because they are made in the image of God; free-dom of conscience before God means that, even when people make bad choices, such freedom is good in itself, independently of what freedom contributes to social welfare, to the enlivening of the life of the intellect, and the like. Reinhold Niebuhr's famous aphorism nicely combines both premises. "Man's capacity for justice makes democracy possible; but man's inclination to injustice makes de-mocracy necessary."[100]

Democracy is a complex network of practices and principles that involve a host of interacting agents in the public square. These practices and principles change with time and space, but the under-lying commitment to representative democracy matters precisely because without such politics we will be at a loss to negotiate the deep differences that arise when we seek to live together in nations across the face of the earth. The only live alternative to resolving our difference by force is to sit down and work out how we are go-ing to live together in relative peace and harmony. Hence, politics is inescapably an exercise in social ethics. The state and its complex institutions exist as an ethical enterprise; they cannot forgo the fos-

[100]Reinhold Niebuhr, *The Children of Light and the Children of Darkness* (New York: Charles Scribner's Sons, 1944), xiii.

tering of virtue, for their very existence is called forth by the need to find a way to live together without killing each other. Thus every effort needs to be extended towards securing as much consensus as possible on the common good, beginning with the simple good of surviving amidst radical differences.

We can expect, to be sure, that, outside the network of moral platitudes without which it is impossible to have any society or state at all, there will be a lively debate as to what constitutes the common good. Citizens can reach agreement on material moral and political proposals even when they disagree on the grounding frameworks that house these objectives. At other times, there will be radical disagreements on material moral and political proposals, even when folk share the same outlook on how to resolve our disputes. At yet other times, there will be disagreement all down the line. Political life will be inescapably messy and conflictual. However, we can and should expect those who enter politics to use the light they currently possess to find a way forward as best they can for all of us.

Christians, of course, may link the light we all need to survive together to their deepest convictions about the created order. Their theistic commitments provide a fertile soil in which reason (including political reason) may flourish and be enriched in a host of ways. They may connect the light of political reason to the light of God that shines through all creation. Theists from other traditions may make similar discoveries for themselves. Moreover, in this arena atheists and secularists may discover that some of their options have undercut and corrupted the life of the mind in ways that will surprise them. The history of Marxism shows only too clearly that atheism has its own unruly history morally, intellectually, and politically. Happily this is not the whole story, for atheists and secularist have also been on the side of the intellectual angels. We all need to keep our wits about us; we all need to do the best we can to provoke one another to good works politically and intellectually.

The Choice Before Us

This is a daunting challenge, as the reaction to Pope Benedict XVI's famous lecture in Regensburg shows all too clearly.[101] His target in that lecture was not Islam but the secularists who were all too

---

[101] The title of his lecture was "Faith, Reason and the University: Memories and Reflections," and was given in the Aula Magna of the University of Regensburg on Tuesday, 12 September 2006.

eager to reduce the life of reason to the empirical, the mathematical, and the narrowly scientific. This kind of narrowness ruled out deep questions about what it is to be human that are inescapable in politics; or it excluded dogmatically and arbitrarily religious options that should be allowed in any fair and open discussion. The Pope was clearly concerned about the poisoning of the intellectual and political wells by secularists who insist on their visions of the mind and its norms as the only viable options. It is inexcusable and astonishing that many Muslims fastened onto one incidental remark that expressed the opinion of an obscure Byzantine emperor, rather than noting that Pope Benedict was creating space for all thoughtful religion in the public square. So the bloody reactions to this lecture shows that the Pope was right to hint that those theists (Islamic and Christian) who undermine the connection between God and the life of the mind can be a menace in politics. So the choice in the social and political arena is not between believers and unbelievers; the choice is between those committed to intellectual persuasion and those committed to terrorism. It is not a matter of faith over against faith, or faith over against unfaith; it is a matter of the use of debate and discussion (and all that goes with these) over against the use of terror and fear.

It is not easy to calculate the Paddy factor in society and politics, but there is one thing we can do: we can see that it is inescapable. We can also see that in its own complex way it is a great blessing and not at all necessarily a curse. This observation applies as truly to terrorism as it does to a host of other political issues and practices.

8

—

The F-Word

There is more than one F-word in the English language. One of them is not used in polite society; another leads into some pivotal questions about the appropriate response of victims to those who have harmed them. I am thinking of "forgiveness".

Facing Forgiveness

Consider these two cases.

Gordon Wilson lost his daughter Marie in the Enniskillen bombing on November 8, 1987. I had known "Mr. Wilson", as we called him, in my own church on Darling Street. I knew his children from Sunday school, even though we came from the other side of the tracks. Marie was twenty when she died and had been a nurse in Belfast. I also had a great affection for Mrs. Wilson, for she played the organ in our church, and she had known my father before he was tragically killed many years before in a bad truck accident. Gordon Wilson was not an especially pious person. One observer described him as a "craggy drapery maker".[102] Indeed some of the more fervent saints around Enniskillen were wont to complain from time to time that he might be a spiritually suspect, for he did not fully share their particular forms of piety, and he was not afraid to let that be known. He had a pronounced southern Irish accent, and he was known in the town as a shrewd and eminently success-

---

[102]Jonathan Stevenson, *We Wrecked the Place* (New York: The Free Press, 1996), 258.

ful businessman.

On the morning of November 8 he had gone with his daughter to stand near the war memorial, watch the parade, and remember the dead from the two world wars. With the other ordinary citizens who had gathered, they had taken the full force of the bomb. He had been injured but survived. His daughter had been killed. She died holding his hand beneath the rubble. She was one of eleven who had been killed that day.

On the day of the bombing I caught the interview with Gordon Wilson on national television. It was crisp and clear. Buried under the concrete, somebody grabbed Gordon Wilson's hand. He described the situation with a minimum of elaboration. In a voice, cracking with emotion, he responded to what was happening.

> It was Marie. Marie said, "Is that you, Daddy?"
> I said, "Yes."
> "Are you all right, Daddy?" she asked.
> I said, "I'm fine."
> Three or four times I asked her if she was all right and each time she replied, "I'm fine, how are you?"
> I said, "Hold on. They will be coming to have us out soon."
> Then she said, "Daddy, I love you very much." That was the last thing she said.
>
> I have lost my daughter, and we shall miss her. But I bear no ill will, I bear no grudge. Dirty sort of talk is not going to bring her back to life. She was a great wee lassie. She was a pet and she's dead. She is in Heaven and we'll meet again. Don't ask me please for a purpose. I don't have an answer. But I know there has to be a plan...it's part of a greater plan, and God is good. And we shall meet again.[103]

On my first visit home to Enniskillen after the bombing I went to see the Wilsons. On meeting Gordon again after being gone for almost two decades, I found a man of extraordinary faith and integrity. He recalled with good humor what had happened when a memorial service for the dead was held in the Roman Catholic Church in Enniskillen. He had entered a packed church to a standing ovation. Instinctively he looked around to see what grand dignitary, like a bishop or archbishop, might be following him. There was no such dignitary; the standing ovation was in his honor. We kept in touch as best we could until his death from a heart attack in 1995.

[103] Gordon Wilson, with Alf McCreary, *Marie: A Story from Enniskillen* (London: Harper Collins, 1900), 46.

In fact, I was the last person to give his son Peter the sacrament of Holy Communion one Sunday evening in the Darling street church before he was tragically killed in a road accident before Christmas 1994. Gordon bore that tragedy too, at least as far as outsiders could see, with great dignity and fortitude. He was appointed to the Senate of the Irish Republic in recognition of his work for peace.

In 1993 Gordon Wilson went on a secret mission to the meet with the IRA to confront them and plead with them to abandon their campaign of terror. They handed him a hand-written apology for the death of his daughter and insisted that the Enniskillen bombing had been a mistake. They were unrepentant, though, blaming the troubles wholly on the presence of the British in Northern Ireland. Coming away from the meeting, he had no illusions.

> I said, I am tired of hearing the IRA talking about their mistakes. And really, it was then agreed that we weren't getting anywhere. Some call me naïve, and said I was made a fool of, and maybe they were right. God knows. But I had hopes. People had told me they couldn't think of anybody more likely to get something from the IRA, in the way of a little peace. I thought I might, if only a change of emphasis. I was wrong.[104]

In March 2006 Rev. Julie Nicholson stepped down as priest-in-charge of St. Aidan with St. George's Church in Bristol. She did so because she could not forgive the killers of her daughter, Jenny, who died in the Islamist terrorist bombings of July 7, 2005, in London. Fifty-six people were murdered that day by Islamist terrorists. Jenny Nicholson, who was twenty-four, was killed by the suicide bomber on the eastbound Circle line service that she had boarded at Paddington station. Over a thousand mourners attended her funeral in Bristol Cathedral, where her mother was too distraught to speak. The flower arrangements around the cathedral were studded with sunflowers, Miss Nicholson's favorite bloom. Jenny was a gifted singer and pianist and had been head chorister at St. Mary's Henbury in Bristol, where her mother had been a curate. One of her last phone calls from Paddington station was to her dad, Gregg, minutes before the bombing. She had a master's degree in Music from Bristol University and worked in London with the Rhinegold music publisher.

Her mother had not been able to return to the pulpit since the

[104]"I Asked The IRA if They Were Prepared for 3,000 More Dead. They Said Yes," *The Times* (London), November 5, 1993, 17.

day of the July 7th bombings. After a period of compassionate leave she had taken up work on a church-backed community youth project. She was forthright in her comments on her resignation from parish work:

> I rage that a human being could choose to take another human's life. I rage that someone should do this in the name of God. I find that utterly offensive. We have heard a lot of things causing certain people offence and I would say that I am hugely offended that someone should take my daughter in the name of a religion or a God. I have a certain amount of pity, the fact that four young men felt that this was something they had to do. But I certainly don't have any sense of compassion. Can I forgive them for what they did? No I cannot. And I don't wish to. I said in the early weeks and still now say the name of my daughter's murderer, Mohammed Sidique Khan, every day. I believe there are some things in life which are unforgivable by the human spirit. We are all faced with the choice and those four human beings on that day chose to do what they did. I leave potential forgiveness for whatever is after life. I will leave that in God's hands. I take Jenny with me every inch of the way so, although physically her body is gone from this world, the essence of her is very much with me in this world. And as long as I have life then the spirit of Jenny will have life. Forgiving another human being for violating your child is almost beyond human capabilities. All my understanding of what it means to be a priest is peace, reconciliation and forgiveness. It is very difficult for me to stand behind an altar and celebrate the Eucharist, the Communion, and lead people in words of peace and reconciliation and forgiveness when I feel very far from that myself. If someone were to say to me that my ability to forgive Jenny's killers would end the violence I could probably find the courage to do it. But I am not sure in my heart I would believe it. Part of my recovery was a search for a way through all this. I have really, really struggled. I have always been in awe and humbled by those who stand up and say from a faith perspective, 'I forgive'. I read more books on forgiveness in the months after Jenny died that I have ever done. A lot of imagery I worked with is of Mary at the foot of the cross and forgiveness doesn't come into it at all. If Jenny had survived, however awful her injuries, and had said 'Mummy, I forgive them' then I would have had to do so as well. But she didn't, she died.[105]

The responses of the Rev. Julie Nicholson and Gordon Wilson take us to the heart of a searing set of problems raised by terrorism.

---

[105]These comments were made in an interview with BBC Bristol and were accessed at http://www.telegraph.co.uk/news/uknews/1512281/Vicar-who-cant-forgive-steps-down-from-pulpit.html, accessed on October, 4 2012.

How do the victims deal with the challenge of forgiveness, reconciliation, justice, and peace? In time I shall work my way through these themes, but we need to make haste slowly.

Clearly Gordon Wilson and Julie Nicholson went through a living hell of their own that observers can barely begin to understand. Even then, they still wanted to do what they could to bring peace to the world that had been so brutal to them. What astonishes and refreshes us in the response of Gordon Wilson is the insistence that there be no "dirty talk." He clearly did not want to see another atrocity carried out in retaliation for the one in Enniskillen. Perhaps he did not want other parents to go through the hell he was going through. What astonishes and refreshes us in the response of Julie Nicholson is her naked honesty and integrity. The juxtaposition exposes the initial dilemma. On the one hand, both of them feel an obligation to forgive and make a contribution to the ending of killing and the onset of peace; and, on the other hand, both display how difficult these tasks are. Forgiving is a lovely idea until we have to forgive. It sounds easy until we have to deal with the loss of a daughter who has been brutally murdered. Seeking peace is a lovely idea until we have to seek peace. It sounds easy until we are faced with the determination and passion of systematic killers. The IRA dubbed the death of Marie Wilson a mistake (there were lots of "mistakes") and after a cheap apology went on their merry way of killing and destruction. Mohammed Sidique Khan killed Jenny Nicholson, died, and headed off to his menagerie of virgins in paradise.

Seeing straight is a challenge in such circumstances. As we dwell on the generosity, we should also dwell on the honesty manifest in the rage and anger of Julie Nicholson. Contrary to popular moral mythology, the vindictive emotions of resentment and revenge are not morally blind. They are not just visceral reactions; they are truth-detecting mechanisms. Just as our admiration detects the goodness of Gordon Wilson, so does the rage of Julie Nicholson detect the violation of the good in the murders of Marie and Jenny. Admiration and rage are both essential if we are to do justice to reality. The journey from rage to generosity may be long or short; but it is a journey where both the starting point and the ending cannot be set aside; the rage and the generosity give us a reading of important features of the universe. Equally, the journey from forgiveness to social peace can be paved by good intentions, but if the curves are not properly negotiated it will lead us further into hell. There are potholes everywhere. Terrorists bomb their way into the peace process; theologians morally coerce their way into the peace process. Killers destroy human life by killing it; many theologians trivialize human life by lack of clarity and delusion; neither knows how to use the F-word properly.

The Logic of Forgiveness

What is it to forgive? To forgive at its most basic means this: abandoning rage and resentment against those who have harmed us, and extending pardon to them for their wrongdoing. In the standard cases there is both a subjective and an objective dimension. Forgiveness on the subjective side means letting go of the hurt and the resentment that naturally arise when others harm us. For this reason there is a therapeutic element of inner healing that accompanies forgiveness, but forgiveness does not stop there. Forgiveness on the objective side means that we extend pardon and release those who have wronged us from their guilt. For this reason we generally forgive by actually saying "I forgive you" to the wrongdoer. This objective dimension is captured in the economic imagery often deployed. We speak of a debt or an interest loan being forgiven; the forgiven are released or absolved from payment. Both dimensions are often seen in the joy and gratitude of those who have been forgiven. They are not just relieved that the one they have harmed feels differently towards them; they are also happy that they have been pardoned. In the paradigm case of forgiveness, both the subjective and the objective are characteristic features of forgiveness.

Is forgiveness in the full sense conditional on repentance? Does it require that the person to be forgiven acknowledge their wrong doing, turn away from it, and even make appropriate restitution where possible? Surely, yes. To be technical, forgiveness is a performative act that is interpersonal and bilateral; there is action by both parties. Minimally in normal cases the person to be forgiven acknowledges the evil they have done and apologizes; the person harmed forgives by saying sincerely, "I forgive you." So forgiveness is an act; it is not a mere disposition. To be sure, one can have a forgiving spirit, that is, a readiness to forgive those who harm us. However, forgiveness should not be confused with a forgiving spirit, or even with a more general disposition to love. Forgiveness involves specific acts of forgiving, dealing with real harm that has been done in contingent circumstances.

There are, of course, anomalies and borderline cases. These anomalies show up in cases where there is death and where there is ignorance. Thus in the case of those who are dead, it makes no sense to speak of forgiving them simply because they are no longer alive. In this instance, when we speak of forgiving them, the weight falls wholly on the psychological element in forgiveness; the whole is allowed to speak for the part. It is this that is clearly to the fore in the honest recognition of Julie Nicholson that she cannot forgive the killer of her daughter. She cannot let go of the rage; here releasing the killer from what he owes her simply does not arise. In the case of those who are ignorant of what they are doing, we can still speak of forgiveness even though there are mitigating circumstances that prevent them from knowing the harm they are doing. Because they do not fully know what they are doing, we find it easier to abandon resentment and to forgo what they owe. Moreover, we can sometimes get beyond agony and resentment by speaking and acting as if the offender is forgiven in the full objective sense of the word.

However, it is mistaken to treat anomalies as standard cases. Standard cases also make it clear that forgiveness is conditional on repentance, and true repentance will lead to repair of the wrongdoing. The normal way to obtain forgiveness is this: the wrongdoer acknowledges the wrong he has done, says he is sorry, indicates that he does not intend to do it again, and asks for forgiveness. If I deliberately ruin your good name by spreading disinformation about you, then the path to forgiveness is obvious. I seek you out, acknowledge the harm I have done, apologize, make it clear that I will cease and desist, indicate that I will undo as best I can what I have done, and ask for forgiveness. Repentance is not preliminary throat clearing; it is crucial to the giving and receiving of forgiveness. Of course, for trivial cases of wrongdoing we relax the conditions; to set them aside in cases of heinous moral evil is to trivialize the evil. Forgiveness, I repeat, is conditional on repentance.

In the Christian tradition the place of acknowledgement is brought home most powerfully in the case of the unforgivable sin. In this critical example we are confronted with those who accuse Christ of being in league with the demonic. They make the cutting comment that Christ is working in league with the devil. They have become so corrupted in their judgment that when confronted with ultimate goodness they perceive it as ultimate evil. They cannot acknowledge their sin and repent because they have blinded themselves to the truth. Clearly forgiveness is conditional upon acknowledgement of evil and upon repentance; they cannot be forgiven because they cannot repent, and they cannot repent because of their obduracy and blindness.

Even when there is acknowledgement of evil and genuine repentance, practicing forgiveness can be a tremendous challenge. The honesty and integrity of Julie Nicholson makes this abundantly clear. At a personal level, it may be virtually impossible to eradicate the suffering inflicted by the offender from one's mind. The pain simply goes too deep. One may even be willing to forgive and want to forgive, but when one comes face to face with the person who harmed us one may fall short of actually forgiving. This fits with the fact that the Christian tradition has always insisted that it is the grace of God that ultimately makes forgiveness possible. Moreover, one can easily have genuine doubts concerning the sincerity and depth of change in the offender.

Once we entertain such doubts, we can also see why it is vital to distinguish between forgiveness and reconciliation. In reconciliation we envisage the restoration of full fellowship with the offender. Forgiveness is clearly essential to reconciliation, but reconciliation goes much further in the restoration of the broken relationship. In fact we can have cases of forgiveness where there is no need for reconciliation, for there was no relationship to begin with. Thus there can be forgiveness between strangers but there cannot be reconciliation between strangers. Reconciliation of the broken relationship cannot take place simply because the relationship never existed. Of course, a new relationship can then begin beyond the act of forgiveness, but beginning a new relationship is quite different from the reconciliation of a broken relationship.

Moreover, forgiveness may or may not lead to personal reconciliation. Reconciliation too is characteristically bilateral; it takes action from both parties to effect genuine reconciliation. The offending party may accept the forgiveness but then rightly decide not to rebuild the relationship. Perhaps they think they have done enough damage and do not want to put further burdens on their victims. The offended party may also demur. Imagine the case of a victim of sexual abuse and rape. Is she morally obligated to have table fellowship with the person who abused her? This is absurd. Even if we were reasonably certain of the offender's repentance and change of heart, it would be morally outrageous to insist on reconciliation. Equally, it would be cruel to ask victims of terrorism to be reconciled to those who have killed their loved ones, least of all when the killers see themselves as heroes who show no signs of remorse and repentance. In fact in these instances it is nonsense to speak of reconciliation because there never was a relationship to reconcile; the victims were strangers picked at random by their abusers and killers.

A Place for Justice and Punishment

What about justice? Does forgiveness and reconciliation cancel out justice? Those who killed Jenny Nicholson are dead; they are beyond the reach of earthly justice. Those who killed Marie Wilson still remain unidentified and free. What should be done if they were to be found and arrested?

Domestic terrorists deserve both the protection and the full weight of the criminal justice system. They deserve protection, for naturally some of those who identify with the injured will want to exact revenge by taking the law into their own hands. This is why Gordon Wilson's insistence that there be no "dirty talk" was precisely correct. Even while being punished for their crimes, terrorists are persons with rights who are not to be used as means to an end. They deserve the respect due to them as persons.[106] However, they also deserve the full weight of the law in punishment, for such behavior is morally reprehensible, and it is rightly outlawed as criminal and punished by the state. The state exists minimally to protect the innocent, to preserve the peace, and to administer justice. It would be morally bizarre in the extreme if terrorist killers were given a free ride when thieves, or rapists, or everyday killers, were hauled off to prison. The romance that still hangs as a grey halo around the heads of terrorists (maybe they are freedom fighters so they should be given the benefit of the doubt) needs to be scuttled with gusto at this point. Justice is an equal-opportunity practice; it is not a beanbag from which we can choose arbitrarily to exclude certain

---

[106]This applies to international terrorists as well, but I shall not deal with the additional ramifications that are at stake in cases of international terrorism.

colored beans.

It is often thought that to forgive also requires that the offended party give up all thought of reparation or punishment. This is mistaken. Our obligations at this level are complex. In cases where no criminal action is involved, if a person deliberately harms another, it is only right that that person be obligated to make reparations where that is possible. If I deliberately smash your car, I should replace it or pay damages. In these circumstances, the person harmed may well forgo reparation, but there is no obligation to do so. In some circumstances such behavior may be heroic, exhibiting a conspicuous goodness that overflows our ordinary moral requirements. In some circumstances, it may well be a demand of the offender that he or she be allowed to make reparation, and this surely should be permitted. Reparation may be very important for the healing and welfare of the offender.

In cases where criminal activity is involved, then the situation is entirely different. Just as a person has no right to take the law into their own hands in order to right a wrong done against them, so a person has no right to waive the requirements of the law when a serious wrong has been done to them. If someone murders your child, you do not get to decide if the accused murderer should or should not be arrested and face charges. Those in power are apt to ignore this when they are under pressure to achieve political ends that will be thwarted if the law takes its course. They can readily reach for language of forgiveness and reconciliation as a way to cover their spin. When such discourse is skillfully presented in quasi-religious settings, it is easy for ordinary people to become confused. The law rightly takes the issue of justice out of the hands of the offended (and of politicians) so that there may be an independent rendering of what is due. To be sure, the agents of the legal system can take into account how things stand between the offender and those offended, but this is a far cry from abandoning the requirements of justice. Forgiveness (and personal reconciliation) and justice are radically different concepts; they stand whole and complete on their own. To deploy forgiveness to undermine justice is to pave the way for further evil.

Justice in these circumstances is to be distinguished from therapy and from deterrence. Both therapy and deterrence can be taken into account in the administration of justice. Every effort can and should be made to heal violent agents of their nefarious dispositions and to deter others from imitating their killing sprees. However, terrorists are first and foremost agents rather than patients. They have chosen specific strategies to execute their intentions; they have even been trained at great cost to themselves and others to develop those strategies. They are not victims; they are full-blooded agents. They deserve appropriate punishment. Lesser crimes merit lesser punishment; greater crimes deserve greater punishment. When their punishment is complete, absent capital punishment, they are then free from state interference. They are once more agents who are to be received back into society. In and through the administration of justice, there is always space both for mercy and for the consideration of mitigating circumstances. This is why justice can never be a matter of simple calculation; it must ultimately be in the hands of judges and juries who can take all the relevant factors into consideration.

To be sure, this sort of analysis has often been challenged. On the one hand, moral and religious sentimentalists think it is harsh and unloving. They want to restrict punishment to therapy or deterrence. Unfortunately, they invariably mistake revenge for retribution; they confuse love with license. They ignore the crucial distinction that exists between a person paying back someone for harming them and a properly constituted system of law holding wrongdoers responsible for what they have done. Reaching merely for therapy or for deterrence ultimately undercuts justice. With therapy and deterrence, there is no end to what can be meted out in their name to agents who deserve their day in court. If we rely merely on considerations of therapy and deterrence, injustice will run rampant, for the punishment will no longer relate to the actual crime committed but to other considerations. Appropriate retribution for those who deserve it is essential to justice. This is not some narrow vision of justice that we can replace at will by some better notion of justice; it is constitutive of justice itself.

On the other hand, some tough-minded post-modernists will be tempted to dismiss all law as the administration of raw power dealt out in the interests of those who control the levers of the system. Such theorists simply fail to distinguish innocence from guilt. For them there can be no morally relevant distinction between the victim and the victimizer, for everything is a matter of power and interests camouflaged as morality and order. Should this vision be implemented, postmodernists would hand us all over to the crude forces of violence that stalk every civilization. It is crucial that we resist being intimated by this academically popular but backhanded attack on justice. In justice the state holds terrorists responsible for their killings and administers appropriate punishment that will deliver fairly what they deserve.

It is very tempting for well-meaning clergy and pious folk to press the necessity of forgiveness and reconciliation without coming to terms with the moral issues involved, most importantly the requirements of repentance and justice. I grew up in Northern Ireland at a time when the main Protestant churches were tempted to take this route. Church leaders often approached the problem laden with shame and guilt. They felt that the troubles and their attendant violence were intimately tied to ethnic and nationalist disputes that were laced in turn with religious content and significance. It was hard to look the press and the world in the face and not sense that church had been grievously at fault. As things got worse, it was natural to sharpen the call for forgiveness and reconciliation both as a solution to then current disruptions and as a compensation for former complacency and complicity. Aside from the fact that calls for reconciliation were nonsense since there was no relationship between killers and victims to reconcile, over time I found that the constant round of calls for forgiveness and reconciliation rang hollow. These repeated calls were supposed to bring about social change; they failed abysmally. As happened in the case of Gordon Wilson's meeting with the IRA, the calls made next to no difference to the situation. Julie Nicholson was right to be skeptical as to whether anything she might say or do would make a whit of difference to radical Islamic terrorists. Indeed the language of peace and reconciliation will be readily co-opted by terrorists. I recall vividly, while staying in a hotel in North Carolina over a weekend, watching a leading terrorist leader dress up his violent political and nationalist agenda so skillfully in the language of inclusion, peace, and reconciliation, that I was morally sick to my stomach. It was virtually impossible to cut through the clever rhetoric and moral fog to get to the real issues at stake. In the case of Islamic terrorists the appeal to forgiveness and reconciliation as a prescription for social change are even less persuasive.

Forgiveness and the Quest for Peace

How do forgiveness, reconciliation, and justice relate to the transitions to normal, civilian life? Do not forgiveness and reconciliation play a critical role in the search for peace in communities that are torn apart by ethnic strife and violence?

We move here from the interpersonal to the communal. We know that in interpersonal situations forgiveness and reconciliation (where it applies) is vital to the achievement of peace and harmony between estranged individuals. We also know that when it comes to one community forgiving another, matters are much more complicated. In modern societies, there are virtually no recognized mechanisms for seeking corporate pardon for offences committed. Communities are made up of a mixture of persons who may or may not join in the relevant acts of repentance and reparation. Communities can change quite drastically over the generations, so that even identifying what communities have done to each other can be subject to debate and suspicion. However, hope springs eternal in the human breast, so should we not develop the idea of forgiveness and reconciliation and put them to work in the political arena in places scarred by terrorism?

The most famous instance of such a development is the work of the Truth and Reconciliation Commission in South Africa. In that case the leadership of the country was between a rock and a hard place. They could go for total amnesty (as is customary after war) or for full punishment (like at Nuremburg), but both of these would have undermined in various ways the delicate transition to the new society that most desperately wanted. So the South African leaders opted for a third alternative. They "granted amnesty to individuals in exchange for a full disclosure relating to the crime for which amnesty was sought."[107] They decided "to balance the requirements of justice, accountability, stability, peace, and reconciliation."[108] Out of 7,112 perpetrators who applied, 849 were granted amnesty. For Archbishop Desmond Tutu such a move was an artful implementation of the African concept of *ubuntu*. *Ubuntu* signifies a deep

[107] Desmond Tutu, *No Future Without Forgiveness* (New York: Doubleday, 1999), 30.
[108] Ibid., 23.

belonging together.

> A person with *ubuntu* is open and available to others, affirming of others, does not feel threatened that others are able and good, for he or she has a proper self-assurance that comes from knowing that he or she belongs in a greater whole and is diminished when others are humiliated or diminished, when others are tortured or oppressed, or treated as if they were less than who they are.[109]

When Archbishop Tutu and others brought news of the success of the Truth and Reconciliation Commission to Belfast, those who listened to his speeches "heard the message as if in a sense it had been uttered by a divine oracle."[110] At the time the big issue in the news was that of the decommissioning of terrorist weapons, but despite failure on that critical front, Archbishop Tutu exhorted his listeners to soldier on in the work of peace and reconciliation. The divine oracle was certainly received with enthusiasm. As Alex Boraine, another member of the commission who visited Belfast, found: "If there is one factor, one truth, that emerged from the visit [he made to Belfast] it is in itself the importance of establishing truth, and as far as possible an agreed truth, as a vital means of moving on from the conflict."[111]

Others have focused less on truth and more on forgiveness as the critical factor in moving towards peace and reconciliation. Alan Torrance, the distinguished Scottish theologian, speaking directly to the situation in Northern Ireland, has insisted that the church has gone badly astray in making forgiveness conditional on repentance. Torrance believes that the Irish churches (Protestant and Catholic) are badly mistaken in the assumptions governing their attitudes to one another.

> The Presbyterian Protestants on the one hand appeal to a theology of election and limited atonement to interpret their "unconverted" opponents as being outside the realm of grace and God's purposes and who therefore are to be understood not in terms of Christ but in terms of God's judgment. Accordingly they go on to interpret their history in this light, in terms of God's deliverance of his faithful from the anti-Christ and his establishing them in their land. The state, its law and its history are not interpreted in terms of Christ in whom all men and women discover their

---

[109] Ibid., 31.
[110] Ibid., 262.
[111] Alex Boraine, *A Country Unmasked* (Oxford: Oxford University Press, 2000), 412.

humanity and that of their neighbor cleansed and made acceptable before God. Rather Christ is interpreted in terms of their own particular perception of their history and country. On the other hand, Roman Catholics, working also with a particularist conception of God's purposes of grace and interpreting the mediatorial role of Christ as restricted to the one true 'catholic' church, interpret the Protestant not in terms of who Christ is and his universal atonement, but in terms of their own very different Republican perception of Irish history and of the state with its ordained function to uphold God's universal natural purposes for man over and against their betrayal in abortion, birth-control and so on. Accordingly, neither party allows their thinking in the socio-political context to be controlled first by God's purpose of grace or by the person of Christ, but rather it is controlled by their own perceptions of their history and of the nature of grace.[112]

Were Irish Christians to follow the truth about nature and grace, Torrance is very certain that they would be drawn to a very different vision of forgiveness. They would no longer see forgiveness as an attitude of mind to be implemented after a dispute has been settled and the legal requirements satisfied; forgiveness would be front-loaded into the whole process.

Forgiveness is not an act so much as an attitude of acceptance operating at the very root of one's apperception ... This forgiving acceptance is never a "private" attitude but necessarily public involving the eyes, the ears, and the mouth as symbols of true humanity. It commits one to see "eye to eye", to communicating forgiving acceptance in what is said and hearing the word of forgiveness as it is spoken.[113]

That context for this grandiose proposal, he insists, is the gospel as represented by the famous parable of the prodigal son. The father is already waiting for the wayward son to come home after spending his inheritance in riotous living. When he returns the father gladly welcomes him back into the family. Forgiveness is logically prior to repentance on a proper understanding of grace, and it is not conditional on repentance. The implications for political forgiveness are obvious.

...the absolute priority of God's love and law must be retained in our involvement in the socio-political context. Forgiveness

---

[112] Alan Torrance, "Forgiveness: The Essential Socio-political Structure of Personal Being," *Journal of Theology for South Africa* 56 (1986), 50–51.
[113] Ibid,. 55 and fn. 10.

does not suddenly become conditional, posterior to the satisfaction of the requirements of justice in the socio-political context ("legal social repentance") but must be there as the ground in which reference to which true repentance ("evangelical, social repentance") can come about, such that justice can be done in the spirit of openness and acceptance of the other.[114]

Torrance goes even further.

...unconditional forgiveness is constitutive of humanity. The bipolar nature of man as person (who finds true being in loving) means therefore that forgiveness simultaneously fulfills the humanity of those who forgive by bestowing humanity on those forgiven. Refusal to forgive unconditionally dehumanizes both parties, establishing individualism and destroying community and the true nature of man as person by way of a legalistic notion of conditional acceptance.[115]

It will come as no surprise in the light of this that Torrance makes exceptionally strong assertions for his claims about forgiveness. It is unconditional forgiveness that alone, he says, can cut through the false stories estranged groups develop about each other; and it is in the context of unconditional forgiveness alone, he insists, that justice is truly discovered and enacted. Unconditional forgiveness will also take us out of the secular individualism that blinds us to the truth made known in Christ. Any other vision of forgiveness will not just be theologically wrong; it will be damaging, sentimental, and irrelevant.

Keeping Our Theological Wits About Us

It is not good form to look a gift horse in the mouth, but when the cat brings home a mouse as a gift, we do not pretend it is a horse. Moreover, if the gift horse is presented with loud fanfares (and government backing) and with promises to be the one and only route to peace in a divided community, we are wise to examine its teeth. Even if a celebrity archbishop and a distinguished theologian bring the horses all decked out in name of the gospel, we should keep our wits about us. I like horses, especially those that have a chance of bringing peace and reconciliation to the social worlds I inhabit. We need all the creative horses we can find. Overall, of the two horses on offer here Tutu's horse is the better one.

Torrance's horse, to put it straightforwardly, is badly bred. When

[114]Ibid.
[115]Ibid., 56.

he says that forgiveness is not so much an act as an attitude, he is confusing a forgiving spirit (and having a loving spirit) with the actual act of forgiveness.[116] Forgiving is an action not simply a disposition. When he insists that a proper vision of grace requires us to think of forgiveness as logically prior to repentance, he is confusing God's unceasing generosity towards us with the clear moral requirements that are tied to forgiveness in scripture. It is very revealing that when Torrance quotes with satisfaction Christ's famous injunction that we should forgive seventy times seven, he conveniently ignores the version to be found in Luke. "... if your brother sins rebuke him, and *if he repents*, forgive him; and if he sins against you seven times in the day, and turns to you seven times, and says 'I repent,' you must forgive him."[117] When he makes unconditional forgiveness essential to being human, he suddenly gives human agents powers that are strikingly inflated, for now by refusing forgiveness to others we dehumanize them and ourselves. It is God who bestows humanity; and it is bizarre to think of ourselves as dehumanizing human agents in any serious theological sense, as if we could destroy the image of God in them.

When Torrance argues that forgiveness can help folk get beyond the stereotypes they have of others, he is right; but this is much more likely to happen if forgiveness is conditional on confession and repentance rather than unconditional. If there is no confession and repentance, then we are in the land of illusion; and the stereotype is likely to be reinforced. When he insists that only the context of forgiveness makes the discovery of justice possible, this claim is empirically false. Justice is achieved every day in the courts without the least mention of forgiveness. When he proposes that those

---

[116]The Rev. David Clements, an Irish Methodist minister, whose father was shot dead outside Ballygawley police station in 1985, succinctly captures what is involved in a forgiving spirit in the following comment. "A forgiving spirit rejects the right to retaliate. It will not consider returning evil for evil. A forgiving spirit takes the deliberate decision not to harbor hostility. The evils of the past are not forgotten, but they are not allowed to dominate the present. A forgiving spirit takes the deliberate decision to return good for evil. A forgiving spirit wants the best for those who have injured us. For the unbeliever this may seem absurd but for the Christian it is profound. It opens up the possibility of not just forgiveness but reconciliation. A forgiving spirit grows out of the knowledge of being forgiven by God in Christ (Ephesians 4:32)." Quoted in Norman W. Taggart, "Methodism and the Troubles," *Catalyst Pamphlet Twelve*, June 2005, 2.
[117]Luke 17: 4.

who hold to forgiveness conditional on repentance are somehow in bondage to secular individualism, he is making up philosophical stories. We can reject Torrance's vision of forgiveness and embrace his vision of human agents as essentially interpersonal agents. When he tries to summarize the vision of nature and grace embedded in the Irish churches, he is making up the historical story to suit his theological agenda. Few Irish Presbyterians hold the views attributed to them; and most Irish Catholics are well aware of the proposals of Vatican II where Christ is heralded as present outside the Catholic Church. This horse of Torrance cannot stand on its feet for long, and it cannot bear the load that has been placed on its back in the search for peace.

Tutu's horse is a much more promising animal. At least it has been put to work and enabled South Africa to move from apartheid to democracy and freedom without the agony of a civil war. Much of that success was tightly tied to the very particular time and space involved. One reason for this is surely the extraordinary efforts that were made to conceptualize what was at stake, not to speak of the administrative arrangements, the generosity of the many victims of violence, and the skill of the commissioners. Tutu, at least initially, is very clear on what was proposed. What was at stake was a very special kind of amnesty. Amnesty is, in fact, the closest analogue that we can find in the public and political arena for forgiveness in the interpersonal arena. There are no mysteries about it, for it is a common practice in the history of war. In prospect and retrospect, amnesty as worked out by the Truth and Reconciliation Commission was probably the best way forward for South Africa.

Tutu's horse wobbles, however, at certain crucial phases of the journey. First, as the infamous case of Winnie Madikizela-Mandela makes clear, even though the Truth and Reconciliation Commission chaired by the charming Archbishop Tutu could get the horse to the water, its members could not get her to drink. The Commission found that her vigilante group, the Mandela United Football Club "was involved in a number of criminal activities including killing, torture, assaults and arson in the community."[118] When confronted with the facts, "Mrs. Madikizela-Mandela disdainfully dismissed almost all the testimony against her as 'ridiculous' and

---

[118]Boraine, *A Country Unmasked*, 256.

'ludicrous.' She hardly turned a hair."[119] In fact, it is silly to think that the only way to get at the truth is to have Truth and Reconciliation commissions. Good newspapers and wily historians may do so as well over time.

Second, we should beware of making too much of romantic notions like *ubuntu*; unique though it is, the content of this notion is not tied to Africa; and in most cases we can capture what is at stake by the idea of the common good. Third, it is false to say that the truth telling and forgiveness will lead to reconciliation. If there was no relationship to begin with, then the issue cannot arise; and sometimes the truth can drive folk apart as much as it brings them together. In Ireland the full truth about Sinn Féin leaders would lead to the collapse of the institutions that are currently in place and that are the only hope we have for a decent future.

Tutu's horse wobbles in a truly illuminating fashion in what he says about justice. He begins well in noting that the Truth and Reconciliation Commission did not ignore justice. Thus the amnesty was in place for a very particular period; and those who did not take advantage of the amnesty offered, or who tried to abuse its generosity, were brought to court and faced the full force of the law. Indeed the amnesty was declared precisely so that in time a proper system of justice could be set up and implemented. He begins to go astray, however, when he suggests that what they were doing was striking a proper "balance between the requirements of justice, accountability, stability, peace, and reconciliation."[120] This is misleading. The truth of the matter is that they were setting aside justice in the interests of the future common good. Justice was sacrificed.

Tutu goes further astray when he proposes that the course taken represented a process of restorative justice, a justice that he sees as superior to retributive justice. Noting that the amnesty was an *ad hoc* arrangement for a specific purpose, he writes:

> One might go on to say that perhaps justice fails to be done only if the concept we entertain of justice is retributive justice, whose chief goal is to be punitive, so that the wronged party is really the state, something impersonal, which has little consideration for the real victims and almost none for the perpetrator. We contend there is another kind of justice, which is characteristic of traditional African jurisprudence. Here the central concern is not

---

[119] Tutu, *No Future Without Forgiveness*, 171.
[120] Ibid., 27.

retribution or punishment. In the spirit of *ubuntu*, the central concern is the healing of breaches, the redressing of imbalance, the restoration of broken relationships, a seeking to rehabilitate both the victim and the perpetrator, who shall be given the opportunity to be reintegrated into the community he has injured by his offense...Thus we would claim that justice, restorative justice, is being served when efforts are being made to work for healing, for forgiveness, and for reconciliation.[121]

Tutu's vision of retributive justice is a caricature; and there is little evidence to support all the wonderful results he thinks his concept of justice secured; but I shall let these matters pass. The deep problem here is that Tutu is no longer balancing justice with restoration of relationships, rehabilitation, healing, and such goods; he is eliminating justice altogether by verbal tricks and illusion. Restorative justice has become a placeholder for a network of praiseworthy social goals; taken together or singly, these do not add up to justice; they are radically different phenomena and should not be confused with them. At this point, we can legitimately compare Tutu to Machiavelli. Machiavelli and Tutu occupy the same moral space: both were prepared to set aside justice in the interests of good order and stability. Machiavelli was prepared to permit the killing of the innocent when the only way forward was to clear the ground and start all over again. Tutu was prepared to let the guilty walk tall and free in order to start all over again. Tutu's docile little mare is draped in religious finery; Machiavelli's big stallion stands up straight, tall and naked.

What Can Be Done Should Be Done

So what should be done if we find those terrorists who killed Marie Wilson and the other ten in Enniskillen? They should be arrested, given a fair trial, and punished for the brutal deaths of innocent civilians. Justice should be done and should be seen to be done. As to forgiveness and reconciliation, these are not the business of the state or of busybody, moralistic neighbors; this is for the victims to resolve. Forgiveness is bilateral; it involves actions on both sides. It does not even arise until there is genuine repentance on the part of the killers. We have no right, nor any duty, to forgive Marie Wilson's killers; this is the prerogative of the victims. Reconciliation takes us into other worlds. On the personal level it cannot arise if, as is

[121] Ibid., 54–5.

likely, there was no relationship in the first place between the killers and those they have bereaved; otherwise, this too is for the victims to resolve. At a minimum we should not burden victims by morally requiring them to enter into serious relationships with heartless creatures who have the morals of sewer rats. To speak of embracing the enemy at this point, with its sexual innuendo, is morally obscene.

As to the communal level, there are a lot of silly expectations that should be abandoned. What we really need is the unconditional practice on all sides of civilized politics; beyond that we will be fortunate if we have peaceful co-existence. Peaceful co-existence rather than the utopian will-of-the-wisp of reconciliation is the default position of communities. As to amnesty, this is a matter of political and legal action to be worked out by the powers that be, taking into account the future good of the community. It would be a travesty if amnesty was withheld from those in the police service who had the murky job of handling double agents but given to those who now sit in high political office, living off the fat of the taxpayers' purse, but trailing blood from earlier careers as lethal terrorists. If amnesty is granted to anybody, we should be absolutely clear about what we are doing: we are not implementing some higher vision of justice; we are sacrificing justice.

Clearly, we need to know how to use those many F-words correctly when we are talking and dealing with terrorists.

9

The Evil We Face

Turning To God

Terrorism is not a reason to challenge God; it is an occasion to look deeper into the nature of evil and to find God.

Terrorism poses a whole host of challenges for the ordinary citizen, for the state, for the church and other religious bodies, and for its many victims. No matter which way we look at it, it poses daunting questions and problems. However, terrorism is not just a nasty affair out there in society that cries out for robust opposition; it is also so horrendous in its scope and intensity that it readily leads us to ask pressing personal questions that call for an answer. Terrorism brings us face to face with the challenge of evil in our midst. There is an existential and spiritual side to it that we can ignore but that we cannot deny. Terrorism raises questions about the nature of evil and about the nature of human beings that are searching and self-involving. How are we to understand the nature of evil manifest in terrorist acts? What does this tell us about ourselves? If human agents can be this bad, is there any hope for human beings? If there is hope, where can it be found?

Terrorism that is motivated by religious convictions does not dissolve these questions; it simply intensifies them. It rids us of the pleasant illusion that religion is a benign affair. It reveals that the human propensity to commit horrendous acts of evil is not cured merely by adding religion to the mix of solutions. In fact, terrorism motivated by religious conviction makes matters worse, in that those who appeal to theology to underwrite terrorist acts are likely to be beyond the reach of reason or persuasion. Appeal to the will of God in this instance trumps the appeal to human reason.

Terrorism does not present any dramatically new dilemma for those committed to the Christian faith. It fits into a challenge that has always been recognized, that is, the trial generated by evil in God's good creation. Terrorist acts are genuinely free acts brought about by human agents; they are not acts of God. Moreover, God can no more create free agents who are predetermined not to do evil acts than he can make round squares, or creatures that walk without feet. This is not a matter of desire or power on the part of God; it is simply that such options make no sense. In a world of genuine human agency and freedom, evil is a real option. Within that range of options, terrorism is one of the many that are open to human beings. The freedom God gives us is not a toy freedom, where we can decide, say, between porridge and boiled eggs for breakfast in the morning. It is a freedom where we can save life or kill it; where we can find ways to live together in harmony or find ways to wreck society; where we can live in civil coexistence with our neighbors or blow our neighbors to pieces. It is a freedom where we can choose a path that makes us into saints or choose paths that make us into terrorists.

Of course, there are still questions of faith that readily detain us. Why does God permit this kind of horrendous evil? Why does God not step in and judge those who do evil here and now and put a stop to their horrendous acts? Why can there not be an accident here or there for those who are setting out to bomb innocent people to smithereens? Why not a few minor heart attacks to knock out the masterminds of terror? Why not arrange a short spasm of cognitive malfunction when a pathological killer is being interviewed for initiation into a terrorist cell so that those in command reject him? These questions sound fine until we reflect on them with care. When we do so it becomes very clear that what we are asking is that our freedom be curtailed. We want a positive freedom where God will step in and stop us when we choose to do something seriously wrong. This is not real freedom; it is a bogus freedom. We would be in a world where we could only perform good acts; it would be a toy world which would undercut the radical either/or of good and evil that marks a world where there are deep rather than rigged choices.

The Superficial Attraction of Atheism

Atheists, of course, set all this aside. They simply abandon belief in God and leave the horrendous evil in place. In the short-term this is a neat way out. I drifted into atheism when I was a teenager. I was raised in the bosom of the church, but its message and practices never made much sense to me. I did try out the faith in a serious way under the influence of a wonderful primary school teacher, Miss Abbott. However, one evening my mother told me to go lock up the chickens in the henhouse; I had a royal fight with a younger brother as to whose turn it was; that was the end of my first efforts to take faith seriously. I had reduced faith to feats of virtue and to individual decision. I had not been sufficiently schooled in the faith; and there was no one to see me through the process of initiation.

When I went off to the hard grind of the local grammar school, Enniskillen's Portora Royal School, and got stuck into the joys of study, I underwent a secret intellectual awakening. Within this I could not make head or tail of an invisible creator; the only things that I thought could be real were things we can perceive by the senses. I remember going to the many funerals that were common in the beautiful countryside of Fermanagh and finding myself staring with stark unbelief when hope of the resurrection was announced at the start of the service. Human beings were simply complicated configurations of matter; we returned to dust and that was the end of it. For a while I had a lingering fear of hell. I can still recall the relief I felt when I worked out that if there is no God, there is no one to send me to hell, so fear of hell was pointless. Once this dawned on me, I was set free to think through what to believe and what to make of my life from the bottom up.

However, becoming an atheist did not solve the problems generated by evil. If you subtract God from the sum of your beliefs, evil does not suddenly disappear; it may become even more conspicuous. In fact I soon discovered that evil posed acute problems that atheism failed to satisfy. If there was one thing that was clear to me it was that evil was as real as tables and chairs and all the other material articles that fill up the physical universe. I met evil in my own soul and I encountered it all around me growing up. It was only later that I learned how to speak aptly about all this; but the core intuitions were as clear as the sun. At one level there is no place for good and evil in a purely material universe. No physical description of the way things are gets within shouting distance of descriptions of events or acts as good or evil. Nor will full physical descriptions of human agents begin to do full justice to the nature of human persons who have consciousness, make decisions, evaluate what is going on around them, fall deeply in love, and ponder the reasons why things are. In fact, if human agents are nothing more than complex configurations of physics and chemistry, then the whole idea of holding them accountable for terrorist acts melts into thin air. If our actions are physically determined, then it is simply incoherent to say that we are good or bad; we simply are what we are, complex, malfunctioning physical mechanisms, and that is the end of the matter.

However, the problem of evil cut deeper than even that for me. I sensed that to leave evil as a purely human phenomena was superficial. Perhaps there is more than meets the eye in evil, I thought. In time I found that the whole notion of the demonic was entirely coherent. Of course, I had no firm idea what this might mean; but at the very least it meant that beyond human agents there lay the possibility of demonic agents who were hideously evil and who lured and trapped human agents into evil. Maybe I was just reaching for a dramatic, metaphorical way of capturing the concrete, brutal reality of evil. Maybe I was infected at this point by the folklore of Ireland. After all, growing up I heard all sorts of wonderful stories about the leprechauns, banshees, and the little people who lived in lonely trees stuck in the middle of fertile fields. If you have heard about these creatures, the demonic just takes you up the scale of being a bit. Perhaps the popular mythology of Ireland provided a fertile soil for the cultivation of conceptual options that otherwise might have seemed daft. Or, maybe that Irish mythology and blarney opened a door into the spiritual world for me. It was not, even, that I believed in the demonic, not at all. Everything hinged on what was or was not possible. It was simply that once I realized that the idea of the demonic was a coherent notion, my atheism began to crumble. If the demonic was a possibility, then there could be more to the universe than the material; and once that door was opened, the possibility of God was standing stark naked before me.

I was in deep intellectual trouble. In fact I remember vividly the very paving stones outside the Salvation Army Hall on the Dublin Road in Enniskillen where all this hit me. I was instantly both scared and mystified. Where was I to go with this discovery? If I could believe in the demonic as a possibility, then I could believe in God as a possibility, and my journey into atheism was immediately halted with a thud. So what was I to do now? I made a policy decision on the spot. I would not shift my ground for the moment; I would stick to my atheism for three months; I would still go to church; but if my atheism were still in place by the end of this trial period, then I would abandon the church and see where my wandering thoughts would lead me. In the meantime I would continue to eavesdrop and listen when people talked or taught about these matters, but not get uptight about it. I still think that this was one of the best decisions I have ever made. There was an inner freedom to search and think that was not governed by emotional turmoil or immediate intellectual pressure.

In this search I was profoundly influenced by the local saints I had known in the life of the church. What struck me was their integrity and goodness. Here the theme of evil worked from the opposite direction. How come these folk managed to be so good? Why did these people show such regard to my widowed mother? How come the church sent the orphan money every three months that was so vital for my mother's budget? More precisely, how come they managed to be so good when they were not aware of being good and roundly denied being good? And how did they overcome evil without boasting or making a big deal about it?

Of course, when I explored this fitfully I was hit by another conundrum. In their faith these local, uncomplicated saints had come to terms with evil, that is, they looked at the world thoroughly realistically. So I discovered that the Christian faith highlighted evil rather than swept it under the carpet. Human beings were not sugarcoated or made into pretend figures; the realism was evocative of a deep understanding of human agents. Moreover, they did not locate the source of evil in their political enemies or religious opponents; they located it deep within themselves. Yet they were not hypocrites, or cynics, or pessimists. They refused to take any credit for the goodness they displayed; they were well aware of the evil within professing believers; and they exuded a strange kind of hope that stretched out to everybody they knew. They insisted that such goodness as they had came not from within them but from this

Jesus figure that was at the heart of the Christian gospel.

Moreover, in and around this Jesus figure, there was more evil. His life and his death were marked, on the one side by a reign of terror where innocent children were liquidated by a tyrant and on the other side by the brutality of crucifixion. In between there were all sorts of encounters with this and that instance of evil, not least with self-righteous orthodox folk whose inner lives were deeply flawed. A tyrant king, who was trapped into honoring a stupid oath by a resentful wife, and by a half-naked dancing stepdaughter, had beheaded Jesus' cousin, John the Baptist. It became quite impossible to keep the haunting figure of Jesus at bay; he got under my skin when I least wanted it because his life and teaching were shot through with a realism about the world and about human nature. Moreover, the story of Jesus was set in the wider theological story of creation, freedom, fall, and recovery. Here, evil was mapped on a wider, cosmic horizon. This was simply part of the background music that was inescapable as I dug deeper. The world was located in a drama of good and evil from start to finish. I remember paying attention to the hymns of Charles Wesley (or rather the hymns unceremoniously *grabbed* my attention) and hearing the drama captured there with exquisite linguistic ingenuity. I also heard it in the sermons. I would get out a hymn book at the start of the sermon, pretend I was reading it; but all the while I was riveted to every word.

Most of all I was confronted with evil and the whole Christian package in and around it by reading a fresh translation of Paul's letters by J. B. Phillips that I found in a paperback book that, fortunately, looked like anything but a bible. This meant that I could read it without my family noticing that I was interested in matters of faith. When folk went off to bed, I would run through the material on my own in front of the fire. I remember working my way fitfully through the book of Romans and other letters of Paul. I simply read them the way I was learning to read the classics of English, French, German, and Latin literature at school at the time. At one level I had no clue what to make of it all. Yet I was convinced that these texts spoke with a bracing depth that was not the product of wishful thinking. Later I found an analogy in the work of the famous Swiss theologian, Karl Barth, which captured my situation exactly.[122] I was like someone peering out a window looking at a crowd staring up and pointing to the sky. I knew they saw something vital, but it was not within my range of vision. So I kept on searching. In the end what I was seeking was staring me in the face: it was the full presence of God incarnate in the life of Christ. God himself had entered the drama of his creation and pulled it back towards its proper dignity and glory. He had come among us through the womb of an innocent, teenage virgin and confronted evil head on from within human existence. The irony was startling. I had become an atheist because I had problems with the immateriality of God; now, as I was bumbling my way into faith, I was confronted with the materiality of God in the midst of human evil in the person of Jesus. It sent intellectual shock waves through my whole being.

The shock waves have continued to reverberate through my mind. As an atheist I was looking at religion from the outside in; now I am working from the inside out. My favorite analogy for the transition involved is geometrical: it is like crossing a threshold. When I was a child we sometimes climbed a mountain close to our home, called Topped Mountain. In fact I was born in the bog below Topped Mountain on the road between Tempo and Enniskillen, and as a teenager it was within sight of our front door. We would take our bicycles, ride around the back of it, and tackle it from the south side. We parked our bicycles in the ditch, and headed up the mountain. The south elevation took the form of a dip in the mountain, as if there was a small crater carved into the side of it; inside it you could see very little as you made your way up. Then as you reached the summit, you crossed a threshold with a brilliant 360-degree view of the whole of the countryside. You had crossed over into a whole new universe. Coming to faith was like entering a whole new world that had nooks and crannies and vistas that are still being surveyed and explored. The line is crossed in coming to faith in Christ. Joined to his people and the resources made available in a host of practices, persons, and materials in the church, we look at the world from the inside out. So you look terrorism in the eye, but you look at it from a new perspective with the eyes of faith.

[122]See Karl Barth, *The Word of God and the Word of Man* (London: Hodder and Stoughton, 1928), 62.

The Utter Shallowness of Atheism

Atheists look at terrorism with the eyes of unbelief. Too many of them cheat at this point. To begin, they think that atheism is just the denial of theism. So if you say no to theism, that's the end of the matter. However, no serious theist is the mere theist of the college textbook. Real theists are Jews or Christian or Muslims; they are not the cardboard, one-dimensional figures that show up in the literature attacking them. Real theists are folk who have been initiated into a whole network of beliefs, values, and practices; to reduce these rich networks to theism is to take the blood out of religion. The arrival of aggressive forms of Islam in the West shows how hollow such moves are; and it shows that there are radically different forms of theism available.

Moreover, even sophisticated atheists rarely unpack what version of unbelief they are offering as an alternative. By settling for atheism as a denial of mere theism, they see no need to spell out the alternative perspective they are offering on the world and on ourselves. Should we become Marxist atheists, or Buddhist atheists, or materialist atheists, or Freudian atheists, or humanist atheists, or Nazi atheists? Or should we become vulgar village atheists, like the man I knew in Cullybackey, Co. Antrim, when I worked there? He would show up at special services to see if the gospel was being preached. The next day when I met up the village he would make fun of faith when it was raining by asking me if the angels had started urinating again. All too often atheists leave us to guess what alternative they are presenting. Beyond this they rarely think that they should defend in any serious way their vision of the world and of evil within it, despite the fact that they constantly rail about the lack of evidence in favor of faith. Somehow we are supposed just to take their word for what they say about the world, about ourselves as human agents, and about the evil we all have to confront. There is a hidden dogmatism below the surface; we are offered this or that brand of atheistic faith without evidence by folk who are constantly blowing and going on about evidence.

There is also an intellectual and linguistic poverty when it comes to dealing with evil. Marxists tend to reduce all evil to economics, tracking its origins and forms to abuse of economic resources. Scientific humanists look to biology or sociology for analysis and explanation. Romantic humanists have little but anarchic individualism to fall back on. Perhaps Freudian atheists hold that all human problems stem from bad potty training. Many atheists, of course, have tried again and again to trace any and all forms of evil to religion, that is, to superstition, ignorance, priest-craft, fear of the afterlife, faith, and any other crumb they can find in the region of this or that faith. This has been something of a public blood sport in the twentieth century. The English may have banned fox hunting, but no one has banned faith hunting. Many atheists have been convinced that once we got rid of religion we would have sunshine and light all around. The story of the modern world has been presented again and again as one of emancipation and enlightenment from religion. The history of ideas, indeed modern history generally, has been told as a story of liberation from faith. In reality it has been the story of moving from faith to idolatry, where this or that brutal vision of the world has been foisted upon us in the name of progress and light.[123] There are indeed very dangerous forms of theism abroad in the world, but the alternative to a dangerous version of theism is not a peaceful version of atheism; it may well be a brutal version of atheism that operates without conscience and constraint. The idea that atheism is a benign alternative to faith is a sick joke to anyone who takes the history of the modern period seriously.[124] It is high time that the high priests of contemporary atheism wised up about the mad aunts and uncles in their basements.

Whatever ultimate vision of the world and ourselves we embrace, we all have to come to terms with evil in our midst. Happily, philosophers have started to take evil seriously. The obvious question that comes to mind at this point is this: What light might faith throw upon the evil of terrorism? What might we say about terrorism if we look at it across the threshold of divine revelation as received in the church?

A Thick Description of Evil

It is no accident that Christian thinkers have worked valiantly to

[123]Michael Burleigh's recent work explores this theme with great skill and depth. See his *Earthly Powers, The Clash of Religion and Politics in Europe from the French Revolution to the Great War* (New York: HarperCollins, 2005), and *Sacred Causes, The Clash of Religion and Politics from the Great War to the War on Terror* (New York: HarperCollins, 2006).

[124]See Jonathan Glover, *Humanity: A Moral History of the Twentieth Century* (New Haven: Yale University Press, 2000), and Susan Neiman, *Evil in Modern Thought: An Alternative History of Philosophy* (Princeton: Princeton University Press, 2002).

provide a deep reading of evil and of terrorism. One of the wittiest depictions of evil generally has come from the pen of a famous lapsed Irishman, that is, from C. S. Lewis, in his brilliant little book, *The Screwtape Letters*. Lewis cleverly captures the way in which the evil of war can turn people towards faith rather than away from it. In one of the letters from a senior demon to one of his apprentices, Screwtape instructs Wormwood about the problem war can be in the work to inhibit faith.

> …I must warn you not to hope too much from a war. Of course a war is entertaining. The immediate fear and suffering of the humans is a legitimate and pleasing refreshment for our myriads of toiling workers…let us therefore think rather how to use, than how to enjoy, this European war. For it has certain tendencies inherent in it which are, in themselves, by no means in our favour. We may hope for a great deal of cruelty and unchastity. But, if we are not careful, we shall see thousands turning in this tribulation to the Enemy, while tens of thousands who do not go so far as that will nevertheless have their attention diverted from themselves to values and causes which they believe to be higher than the self ... Consider too what undesirable deaths occur in wartime. Men are killed in places where they knew they might be killed and to which they go, if they are at all of the Enemy's party, prepared. How much better for us if all humans died in costly nursing homes amid doctors who lie, nurses who lie, friends who lie, as we have trained them, promising life to the dying, encouraging the belief that sickness excuses every indulgence, and even, if our workers know their job, withholding all suggestions of a priest lest it should betray to the sick man his true condition. And how disastrous for us is the continual remembrance of death which war enforces. One of our best weapons, contented worldliness, is rendered useless. In wartime not even a human can believe that he is going to *live forever*.[125]

Lewis captures here what we surely all know by now, that is, the experience of violence does not naturally drive us to atheism; it rattles our secular and prosaic conventions.

As to the evil of terrorism the best place to look for deep analysis is to Russia, the home of modern terrorism, where Fyodor Dostoyevsky and Aleksandr Solzhenitsyn have provided searing analyses of its nooks and crannies.[126] Dostoyevsky's novel, *Demons*, is an

---

[125] C. S. Lewis, *The Screwtape Letters* (San Francisco: HarperCollins, 2001), 22–24.

[126] For a chilling overview of terrorism in Russia see Anna Geifman, *Thou Shalt Kill: Revolutionary Terrorism in Russia, 1894–1917* (Princeton: Princeton University Press, 1993).

extraordinary psychological and spiritual account of the mind-set of terrorism as it developed in nineteenth century Russia. It is no surprise that contemporary students in the social sciences have turned to it for insight.[127] Charles Taylor, the distinguished Canadian philosopher, describes *Demons* as

> one of the great documents of modern times, because it lays bare the ways in which an ideology of universal love and freedom can mask a burning hatred, directed outward onto an unregenerate world and generating destruction and despotism...[This leads] young people to political extremes, to a strong ideology of polarization, in which one recovers a sense of direction as well as a sense of purity lining up in implacable opposition to the forces of darkness. The more implacable, even violent the opposition, the more the polarity is represented as absolute and the greater the sense of separation from evil and hence purity.[128]

The challenge of terrorism is in the end one element in the larger challenge of evil in the world. Everything hinges on how we spell out the descriptions we want to deploy. Both Lewis and Dostoyevsky reach for the language of the demonic in an effort to take seriously the full depths of what is at stake. We are reminded of the description of evil that readily cropped up during World War II when folk felt it was as if the end of the world had come and that all hell had broken loose on the earth. Clearly they were drawing on the language of faith; prosaic descriptions simply were not sufficient.

Moreover, it was not as if we are in search of language that makes us look good and the enemy bad. Experience of evil can bring home some very painful truths about ourselves as both agents and victims of evil. Winston Churchill, when he realized what the Allied Armies were doing to German civilians, was once heard to exclaim: "My God! Have we become beasts?" Aleksandr Solzhenitsyn's reflections go even further.

> Looking back, I saw that for my whole conscious life I had not understood either myself or my strivings. What had seemed for so long to be beneficial turned out in actuality to be fatal, and I had been striving to go in the opposite direction to that which was truly necessary to me. But just as the waves of the sea knock the inexperienced swimmer off his feet and keep tossing him back on the shore, so also was I painfully tossed back on dry

[127] See Nina Pelikan Straus, "From Dostoevsky to al-Qaeda," *Common Knowledge* 12 (2006), 197–213.

[128] Quoted in Straus, "From Dostoevsky to al-Qaeda," 206–7.

land by the blows of misfortune. And it was only because of this that I was able to travel the path which I had always really wanted to follow.

It was granted to me to carry away from my prison years on my bent back, which nearly broke beneath its load, this essential experience: how a human being becomes evil and how good. In the intoxication of youthful successes I had felt myself to be infallible, and I was therefore cruel. In the surfeit of power I was a murderer, and an oppressor. In my most evil moments I was convinced that I was doing good, and I was well supplied with systematic arguments. It was only when I lay there on the rotting prison straw that I sensed within myself the first stirrings of good. Gradually it was disclosed to me that the line separating good and evil passes not through the states, nor between classes, nor between political parties either—but right through every human heart—and through all human hearts. This line shifts. Inside us, it oscillates with the years. And even within hearts overwhelmed by evil, one small bridgehead of good is retained. And even in the best of all hearts, there remains…an unuprooted small corner of evil.[129]

Descriptions determine how we will think of solutions. Diseases determine remedies. If we see the world in purely scientific categories, then off to science we will march. If we see the world primarily in political categories, then we will take the first taxi available to the politics department. If we see it fundamentally in psychological categories, we will book a session with the psychiatrist and make a phone call to the therapist. If all we think is at issue is war, we will turn to the military; if it is all a matter of economics, we will wheel out our commitments to socialism, capitalism, and the like. Terrorism cuts to a deeper level than any science can give us; it makes us think about life itself, about human agents, about ourselves, as a problem.

The natural place to go at this point is to the spiritual and the theological. We are in search of a suitable diagnosis and solution to what we think has gone wrong at the very core of our being. However, it cannot be full steam ahead at this point; we need to pause immediately. We cannot simply take the first theological diagnosis and solution that flits across our minds or across the television screen; we can be fooled theologically just as we can be fooled about a host of other matters. Moreover, turning to the theological is fine

---

[129]Edward J. Ericson, Jr. and Daniel J. Mahoney, eds., *The Solzhenitsyn Reader* (Wilmington, De.: ISI Books, 2006), 265–6.

and dandy if we are dealing with communist and fascist terrorists, but not if we are dealing with terrorists who are driven by their theology and their religious practice. Terrorists who have their own theology ready to hand have their own schema of problem and solution. So when terrorism shows up in the costume of religion then we are really in a fix, for now terrorism has become divine. So should we rebook those cancelled flights back to the scientific, the political, the psychological, the military, and the economic? If we are thinking of booking flights at all, rather than go back to these wearisome solutions, we should switch airlines.

The Concept of the Demonic

What we need at this point, I propose, is the concept of the demonic. Lewis and Dostoevsky are exactly right in the direction they want to take us. We were correct to move to the theological and the spiritual; any move back to the secular shows that the secular customs officers have confiscated our theological bags and stripped us of their treasures. Once we find the place where they have dumped them, we can retrieve them and put them to work again. So how do we proceed from here? More precisely, what do I mean by the demonic and how does that notion help? The core issue is this: with the demonic we are dealing with the inversion of the good. Everything is turned upside down and distorted, so that we are deceived in our perceptions and our actions.

With the demonic, we encounter evil masquerading as good, the ugly presenting itself as beautiful, the corrupt in the appearance of purity, and the demonic disguised as the divine. We are visited by idealism that turns out to be destruction, gentleness that becomes sadistic, freedom that ends in despotism, and love that turns out to be hatred. Here, truth is found by intimidating honest observers and killing critics. Honor is gained by killing the innocent. Liberty is achieved by multiplying victims. The renewal of Western society is brought about by the disaffected and the alienated. The emancipation of women is ushered in by radical subordination to men. God's will is executed by the destruction of Jews. Lucidity comes by suppressing debate and intimidating scholars. Peace is accomplished by bloody massacres. Marriage is made sacred by multiplying temporary wives for soldiers. Justice is planted by the use of terror. The highest evil is found by reaching for the highest good.

What is at stake is distortion and deception.

I am well aware that, if we think of the demonic at all, we tend to think of cases of demon possession. The gospel narratives and the history of the church have a steady set of examples that fit this pattern. Most folk, if they are aware of this material, readily dismiss it as legendary, mythology, misdiagnosis of mental illness, and the like. However, the notion of demonic possession is not one that we need address here.[130] Terrorists are not demon possessed, so we can set that notion of the demonic aside. However, that is not the only conception of the demonic. There is an equally legitimate conception of the demonic where we seek to capture a pattern of evil that is a matter, not of demon possession but of initial good intentions, distortion, and deception. In this usage of the term we have a long-standing way of getting below the surface of human action to unpack its hidden springs and trace its seductive allure. It is not that we are for a moment eliminating human responsibility, so that terrorists can dismiss criticism by appeal to the old adage that the devil made them do it. On the contrary, we are charting how human agents start out with the best of intentions in the world and then by degrees wander into self-deception, false consciousness, and radical evil.

The best way to see this is to spell out what is at stake when we say that terrorism is demonic. Consider what is involved in being a top-flight terrorist. Start out by becoming a charismatic figure hiding somewhere in a cave in an obscure and inaccessible corner of the world. Then convince thousands of literate and illiterate young men and women that you are the builder and maker of true civilization. Surround yourself with an adoring network of brothers who are bound together by the shedding of innocent blood. Train young men to commit suicide by the promise of sensual delights in the world to come. Spend your own personal fortune and additional millions of dollars collected in the form of religious charity in the service of the poor. Become such a spectacular organizer of the deaths of thousands of innocent people in a far-away city that your image and name are an icon of purity across a world of piety and faith. Find agents who will seek out and find the nuclear weapons that you can use to burn additional thousands in an incinerating

---

[130]For an interesting exploration of this notion by a psychiatrist see M. Scott Peck, *Glimpses of the Devil* (New York: Free Press, 2005).

fire. While you are at war in a country that you want to use as a basis for training, give permission for your soldiers to be issued blank marriage certificates signed by religious leaders and encourage them to take wives during battle so that they will be sexually fulfilled. Turn marriage, at least in the short term, into a license to rape. The recipe for distortion and deception is straightforward. Let the anti-hero become a hero. Let the pious man step forth as a lethal killer. Offer up sacrifice, death, loyalty, and personal risk in the service of bombs and bullets. Proclaim murder and mayhem as the pathway to life and liberty. Turn noble things upside down and claim to exemplify a life of divine virtue. We have here an instance of the gold standard of classical demonic activity: the inversion of the good, distortion, and self-deception.

Standard secular discourse about terrorism cannot adequately capture the darkness and paradoxes involved. We are bombarded with platitudes. "9/11 was a secret plot by President Bush and his capitalist associates in the White House to provide a pretext to invade Iraq to get more oil." "9/11 was the judgment of God on America for permitting promiscuity and homosexuality." "America has gotten what was coming to her." "The real problem is Fundamentalism." "Terrorism is the natural result of commitment to moral absolutes and the quest for certainty." "Terrorism is all a matter of propaganda of the deed." "It is a blow-back against globalization and American imperialism." "It is a clash of civilizations." We all have our own favorite formula.

The objection to these kinds of explanations is not simply that they are superficial and contradictory. The problem is that this kind of talk is so reductive. It is clear that factors like hatred of the West, the presence of American soldiers in the Holy Land of Islam, belief in sweet sensual pleasures in the world to come, and the like, matter in understanding Islamist terrorism. However, these do not begin to do justice to the fantasies, the sadism, and the erotic attachment to anti-heroes involved. They do not come to terms with the keenly sought after suicides, and the upside-down world that is so readily visible below the surface. The problem is that such terrorists have inverted the good and become subjects of their own distortions and self-deception. This is nothing new in the history of the world. Islamism, a deep perversion of Islam, is one more addition to a long list of demonic forces and ideas that have gripped the modern world. Their name is legion: scientism, positivism, communism, nihilism, Marxism, fascism, nationalism, racism, and materialism. What all of these have in common is their denial of God and their practice of idolatry. They deny God's creation and its meaning, filling up the vacuum with fantasies that promise us life but deliver the death of the soul and all too often the death of the body. They buy into distorted visions of the human condition and deceive themselves into accepting their false promises.

To speak of the demonic here is not to eliminate human responsibility or to shut down our normal quest for explanations. Terrorism is as contingent as the agents who lead it, the motives that drive it, the context that feeds it, and the history that lies behind it. These diverse elements must be mapped with care. However, given the range and depth of terrorism we face, we are driven to see a deeper dynamic at work that takes us beyond our ordinary readings of actions and events. It is at this deeper level that we reach for the concept of the demonic so as to find an illuminating way to capture what is at stake. In appealing to the demonic, I am not here falling for a version of the old heresy of Manichaeanism, as if creation itself were infected. Nor am I saying that the very essence of human nature has been destroyed; on the contrary what is at issue is the radical distortion of the image of God in human nature. More importantly, the appeal to the demonic as a way of getting below the surface implies that there is hope in the picture. In speaking of the demonic we are signaling that we have entered into the order of creation, freedom, fall, and redemption. Once we grant the demonic, a door has been cracked open towards God. If we are open to the demonic, we have to be open to the divine for the demonic is, after all, part of the fallen creation of God.

Consider at this point the remarkable comment of Lieutenant General Romeo Dallaire after his tour of duty with the UN in Rwanda, where he had witnessed such atrocities that he nearly lost his mind when he came back home to Canada.

> After one of my many presentations following my return from Rwanda, a Canadian Forces padre asked me how, after what I had seen and experienced, I could still believe in God. I answered that I know there is a God because in Rwanda I shook hands with the devil. I have seen him, I have smelled him, and

I have touched him. I know that the devil exists, and therefore I know there is a God.[131]

Deliverance Through a Crucified God

We began the most recent leg of our journey tackling head on the appearance of terrorism in the guise of religion. Far from being a reason to look away from the divine as a pathway for illumination, we found that terrorism turned us more deeply towards the divine. What is at stake in terrorism is the inversion of the good, distortion, and deception. While terrorism requires us to work at a host of levels in order to contain and eliminate it, the antidote to it at this deeper level takes us back from the demonic to the divine. At this higher altitude it is a grave mistake to use, say, politics and the military, as a laborsaving device. We need to turn head on to the spiritual and the theological. Given that we are confronted with a much deeper spiritual and theological challenge, it is not enough to change gears; we need to change the vehicles.

We need to pick our vehicles carefully. We can readily imagine the kind of religious answers that many will seek to enlist. Surely, some will say, we now need to shape up and obey divine law. These folk pin their hopes on a new round of divine jurisprudence that will straighten out the world. Others will insist that we now need to find the one and true divine orthodoxy that will set out the truth for us once and for all. Others will direct us to the right institution, or to the right book, or to the right guru, or to the right spiritual technique, or to the latest spiritual prophet to show up on their radar screen. These are much too prosaic and superficial to work.

If the problem is complex and full of paradoxes, we should expect the solution to be no less complex and paradoxical. We need a divine figure whose healing grace can match the whirlwind of inversion that is central to this kind of fall into evil. We need to find the way, the truth, and the life that will stand us up aright and enable us to love God and our neighbors. We need a restoration of the image of God in human agents. We need to be born again through a birth from above and introduced to the moral energy that will take us out of our distortion and self-deception.

We are what we eat. We have digested the poison of the serpent;

---

[131] Lt. Gen. Romeo Dallaire, *Shake Hands with the Devil* (New York: Carroll and Graf, 2004), xxv.

it is time to feast on the bread of heaven. We have devoured the flesh and drunk of the blood of our fellow sisters and brothers; we now need to eat the flesh and drink the blood of the Son of God. It is God alone who can heal us. More precisely, it is not just any God who can save us. It is the God of suffering love who lived and died among us. It is the God who was on Herod's hit list when he massacred the innocents. It is the God who was interrogated by Pilate, the cynical politician preoccupied with questions of security. It is the God who was brutally crucified by Roman soldiers. It is the God who through suffering has judged our evil ways for what they are. It is the God who has gone beyond suffering to defeat the horror of death in resurrection. It is the God who by his Spirit can raise us from the dead and take possession of our hearts and minds. It is the God who knits us into his own body and therein makes available through space and time the treasures of medicine that heal us of our evil ways.

No state, or nation, or religion, or institution, or book, or academic expert, or politician, or philosopher, or guru, can supply what we need at this level. These cannot resolve the paradoxes that haunt us in the knowledge of ourselves brought home by terrorism. Only a new set of paradoxes that match the reality of terrorism can do that. Only a crucified God can deliver us from the demonic. Consider the paradoxes captured with pleasing simplicity in the liturgy for the burial of Christ.

> We see a strange and fearful mystery accomplished today.
> He whom none may touch is seized.
> He who looses Adam from the curse is bound.
> He who tries the hearts of men is unjustly brought to trial.
> He who closed the abyss is shut in prison.
> He before whom the hosts of heaven stand, with trembling stands before Pilate.
> The Creator is struck by the hand of His creature.
> He who comes to judge the living and the dead is condemned to the cross.
> The Conqueror of hell is enclosed in a tomb.
> O Thou, who has endured all things in Thy tender love,
> Thou hast saved all men from the curse,
> O long-suffering Lord, glory to Thee![132]

Every age of the West has its own hour of decision and destiny. In

---

[132] *Vespers of Holy Friday* (Syosset, New York: Orthodox Church in America, 1982), prepared by David Anderson and John Erickson, 24–25.

the nineteenth century we faced the intellectual and political challenges thrown up by Darwin, Freud, Nietzsche, and Marx. In the twentieth century we faced the threat posed by Hitler and Stalin. It was a commonplace of the last generation that, whatever the options we would face in the twenty-first century, they would be entirely secular in nature. We could not have been more wrong. The really big decision is no longer simply between Nietzsche, Darwin, Freud, Marx, Hitler, and Stalin. We must also take into account afresh the challenges posed by Muhammad and Jesus Christ.

If we take the challenge of Jesus Christ seriously, then terrorism is not a reason to challenge God; it is an occasion to find God hanging on a cross and to find there mercy and hope for ourselves, for our enemies, and for the world.

Index

Printed in Great Britain
by Amazon.co.uk, Ltd.,
Marston Gate.